SpringerBriefs in Cybersecurity

T0212021

For further volumes:
http://www.springer.com/series/10634

Cybersecurity is a difficult and complex field. The technical, political and legal questions surrounding it are complicated, often stretching a spectrum of diverse technologies, varying legal bodies, different political ideas and responsibilities. Cybersecurity is intrinsically interdisciplinary, and most activities in one field immediately affect the others. Technologies and techniques, strategies and tactics, motives and ideologies, rules and laws, institutions and industries, power and money—all of these topics have a role to play in cybersecurity, and all of these are tightly interwoven.

The SpringerBriefs in Cybersecurity series is comprised of two types of briefs: topic- and country-specific briefs. Topic-specific briefs strive to provide a comprehensive coverage of the whole range of topics surrounding cybersecurity, combining whenever possible legal, ethical, social, political and technical issues. Authors with diverse backgrounds explain their motivation, their mindset, and their approach to the topic, to illuminate its theoretical foundations, the practical nuts and bolts and its past, present and future. Country-specific briefs cover national perceptions and strategies, with officials and national authorities explaining the background, the leading thoughts and interests behind the official statements, to foster a more informed international dialogue.

Rebecca Wong

Data Security Breaches and Privacy in Europe

 Springer

Rebecca Wong
Nottingham Law School
Nottingham Trent University
Nottingham
UK

ISSN 2193-973X   ISSN 2193-9748 (electronic)
ISBN 978-1-4471-5585-0   ISBN 978-1-4471-5586-7 (eBook)
DOI 10.1007/978-1-4471-5586-7
Springer London Heidelberg New York Dordrecht

Library of Congress Control Number: 2013949629

Foreword

Over the past several years, security breaches, data leakage and cybercrime have risen sharply in Europe. A large percentage of the breaches have been made by insiders, such as employees, partners and contractors. A number of threats and successful attacks (virus. worms, botnets, etc.) have also been launched by outsiders and organised criminal elements resulting in phantom Internet credit card transactions, and growing reports of data breaches, especially in the medical and banking sectors. Organisational efforts to manage security have mostly been focused on external threats—the hackers, fraudsters and money launderers who exploit weak spots in the organisation's defence—laying minimal focus on internal vulnerabilities and threats from the inside. As well as the systems that fail, many systems just do not work well enough, mainly due to the organisation's failure to make adequate investments in security implementations. Numerous companies still do not have security policies and the security policies that are in place are often ineffective. Organisations are also reluctant to report security breaches, fearing possible loss of reputation.

Digital information is fundamental to life today with almost all corporate data now stored electronically. When virtually all tools of our lives are reliant on computer networks, the direct costs of security breach to individuals and companies have increased and necessitated legal and organisational safeguards, which cannot be achieved by technology alone. It is becoming more difficult for organisations to ignore the security and data breaches. A significant aspect of protection requires laws and regulations, which advocate and mandate security processes, data protection and breach reports. European legislators have been galvanised to enact laws to strengthen information and data security, and manage data security breaches, which are important to business credibility and consumer confidence. Citizens need assurance on how their personal data are being protected.

Under the EU ePrivacy Directive (2002/58/EC), when a personal data breach occurs, the provider has to report this to a specific national authority, usually the data protection authority or the communications regulator "without undue delay". The provider has to also inform the subscriber or individual directly if there is a risk to personal data or privacy. The data breach notification stands as a buzzer for data subjects. It serves as a warning about the dangers that stem from having personal data compromised. However, while the directive only applies to "providers of publicly available electronic communications services" (mainly telecom operators and ISPs), a limited number of EU Member States implemented the ePrivacy directive with a much broader scope. To ensure that no lacunae or loopholes arise in the divergent implementation of the law, the EU Commission adopted a Regulation on the measures applicable to the notification of personal data breaches under Directive 2002/58/EC on privacy and electronic communications on 24 June 2013. The Regulation has direct effect and aims to harmonise the notification of data breaches by telecommunications companies and internet service providers. The Regulation provides the necessary consistency across the EU so businesses don't have to deal with a complicated range of different national schemes.

The European Commission has also proposed a directive that aims to impose new measures to ensure a high common level of network and information security across the EU. The proposed cyber security would require public authorities, health sector organisations, entities that operate critical infrastructure, banking and credit institutions, cloud computing, transport carriers and social networks, amongst others, to report notification of potential security risks. It will also require actual incidents to be reported to cyber security authorities that will be established across Europe.

This book provides an essential review and update of data protection law and guidance and the legal aspects of information security matters. It describes information security and data breach notification requirements included in the Data Protection Directive, proposed EU data protection regulation, as well as the related cyber-security legislations. Authored by Doctor Rebecca Wong of Nottingham Trent University, the book provides guidance in these areas that are undergoing a period of rapid development.

I am pleased to recommend this book to readers, especially to those who are looking to understand the important legal aspects of data protection, data breach notification and cyber security in the European Union. These are truly invigorating times for the data protection world and thus compel us to keep pace with the evolving legislation, and the diversity of challenges facing cyber-security.

Sylvia Kierkegaard

Contents

Chapter 1
Introduction

It is all about trust and transparency

Cybersecurity Summit, London 2011

The debate is not security versus privacy. It's liberty versus control

Bruce Schneier

Abstract This chapter will set the context and aims of this book which is the extent to which data security breaches play a role within a data protection context. This chapter will introduce and consider the notion of cybersecurity in the context of data protection.

Keywords Cybersecurity • Trust and security • Cybersecurity treaty

"Trust and security" were the words that resonated at the recent East West Institute Cyber Security Summit held in London in 2011 [1]. Whilst discussing the need for a Cyber Security Treaty, there was consensus amongst Government bodies and policy makers that cybersecurity was an issue that needed to be addressed. Amongst the examples in support of a call for a Cybersecurity Initiative, the following examples (not exhaustive) were given:

> Is it acceptable for one country to attack another hospital's database? How about the flight systems that support passenger planes in the air? [2]

Whilst these examples may seem remote with culpability normally attributed to the individual(s) rather than the collective responsibility of a State for the actions or inactions in the event of a cybersecurity breach and criminal sanctions imposed where appropriate (see the UK Computer Misuse Act for instance), it is indicative

Dr. Rebacca Wong—Lecturer at Nottingham Law School. She can be contacted at r.wong@ntu.ac.uk. Grateful acknowledgements to Dr Marco Roscini and anonymous reviewers for theirinsights and feedback into this field. Any errors or omissions remain with the author.

of the concern for discussion amongst cybersecurity issues by experts, corporations and governmental officials around the world.

Discussion about data protection issues and its role arose very briefly. The Data Protection framework within Europe remains a key focal point in understanding how best to achieve a balance between an individual's right to their privacy whilst protecting right to freedom of expression. Information security in the data protection context is more concerned with security breaches involving the loss of data held for instance on a CD or a database resulting in calls from the Data Protection Regulatory Authorities (see UK ICO [3] as an example) for stronger legislative remedies for individuals to deal with Information Security setbacks (see UK ICO [3] and Germany [4, 5] as an example).[1]

This SpringerBrief will consider the notion of cybersecurity in the context of data protection. By this, one is referring to "data breach notification and data security breaches". This will be followed by a detailed analysis of data security provisions under the Data Protection framework by revisiting the background into the Data Protection Directive 95/46/EC and the Directive on Privacy and Electronic Communications 2002/58/EC (as amended by the Citizens Directive 2009/136/EC). The author will then consider the proposed data breach notification provisions introduced under the Data Protection Regulation on January 2012, the UK ICO's response and the European Parliament's proposed amendments followed by a consideration of the Directive against Information system and the proposed EU's draft of the Cybersecurity Directive introduced in January 2013, which is a significant development and its shortcomings.

References

1. EastWest Institute (2011) The second worldwide cybersecurity summit. http://www.ewi.info/second-worldwide-cybersecurity-summit. Accessed 4 Dec 2011
2. EastWest Institute (2011) Protecting the digital economy: the first worldwide cybersecurity summit in Dallas. http://www.ewi.info/dallas
3. ICO (2013) Notification of data security breaches to the information commissioner's office. http://www.ico.org.uk/~/media/documents/library/data_protection/practical_application/breach_reporting.ashx. Accessed 9 April 2013
4. Day J (2009) Germany strengthens data protection act, introduces data breach notification requirement. http://www.jonesday.com/germany-strengthens-data-protection-act-introduces-data-breach-notification-requirement-10-26-2009/. Accessed 26 October 2009
5. Hunton and Williams Privacy and information security blog (2011) German DPAs publish comprehensive FAQs on statutory data breach notification requirement. http://www.huntonprivacyblog.com/2011/05/articles/german-dpas-publish-comprehensive-faqs-on-statutory-data-breach-notification-requirement/. Accessed 31 May 2011

---

[1] This compares with the opposite scenario where individuals willingly share their personal information with friends and colleagues onto a public platform such as social networking website with a different level of privacy expectation. This is not the focus of this chapter.

Chapter 2
Data Protection Directive 95/46/EC

Absract This chapter will consider the background of the Data Protection Directive what it provides in the context of data security breaches. As data security breaches are covered under Art.17 of the Data Protection Directive, the provision will be considered in more detail with reference to recent examples involving data security breaches.

Keywords Data protection directive • Data security breaches

The Directive remains the cornerstone for the protection of personal data in Europe. Although still relatively new when compared to other Treaties such as the European Convention of Human Rights and the Treaty on the European Union [1], the passage towards its implementation has not been without its difficulties. In 2003, the European Commission examined the status of EU Member States and the extent to which they implemented the Data Protection Directive [2] and whilst it has broadly achieved its aim to ensure the protection of privacy, there were differences in the interpretation of the Data Protection Directive by EU Member States which needed to be addressed. The main provision that deals with security issues is Art. 17 of the Data Protection Directive 95/46/EC. At its basic level, it requires organisations to implement technical and security measures to ensure that data is safeguarded against potential breaches by unauthorised bodies.

In the UK for instance, there is the ISO 27000-1 Information Security,[1] which organisations can sign to, but is not mandatory to ensure that access is limited to a certain persons. The main risks through security breaches were identified by the ICO [3] including identity fraud; fake credit card transactions; mortgage fraud and so on.

---

[1] See Cagnazzo, L., P. Taticchi., F. Fuiano, Impacts of ISO 9000 on business performances: a literature review at http://unipg.academia.edu/LucaCagnazzo/Papers/193302/Impacts_of_ISO_9000_on_Business_Performances_a_Literature_Review, last accessed 21 October 2011. ICO, (at http://www.27000.org/), last accessed 4th January 2013.

R. Wong, *Data Security Breaches and Privacy in Europe*, SpringerBriefs in Cybersecurity, DOI: 10.1007/978-1-4471-5586-7_2, © The Author(s) 2013

Perhaps, the question is whether the Data Protection Directive as it stands is rigorous enough without further need for any changes? Whilst Art. 17 of the Data Protection Directive sets out the minimum standards to be adopted in safeguarding the security of data (held by data controllers), the issue was brought to the forefront on the legislative agenda (at least in the UK and European level) when incidents involving data security breaches led to the loss or theft of discs containing individuals' personal data.[2] The frequent occurrence of data security breaches between 2007 and 2008[3] highlight the lack of awareness for information security training and the ignorance (either intentional or not) of basic minimal information security standards and the consequences (from a legal, financial and emotional perspective) arising from data security breaches.

Gleaning from the latest data on security breaches, over 800 data security breaches have been reported in the UK in 2 years.[4] According to the UK ICO, mistakes account for 195 of the 818 data security breaches since November 2007.[5]

In the latest changes to the Directive on Privacy and Electronic Communications 2002/58/EC through the Citizens Directive 2009/136/EC, communication providers are required to report data security breaches.[6] At present, this is limited to communications providers and there is *no* obligation for other sectors (such as the financial sector) to notify data security breaches to national Data Protection Authorities. Data security breaches involving huge data losses such as that of Sony was well-publicised and reported.[7]

---

[2] BBC news. Timeline: child benefits records loss available at http://news.bbc.co.uk/1/hi/7104368.stm, dated 25 June 2008; Leydon, J. Information security breaches quadrupled in 2007 available at http://www.theregister.co.uk/2008/01/02/data_breaches_skyrocket/, dated 2 January 2008.

[3] See footnote 2.

[4] ICO. Report data breaches or risk tougher sanctions, warns the ICO available at www.ico.gov.uk/~/media/documents/.../data_breaches_260110.ashx, dated 27 January 2010. See latest guidelines issued by the ICO on Data security breach management available at www.ico.gov.uk/.../data_protection/.../guidance_on_data_security_br..., dated July 2011. For a background into information security, see Moore, T., R. Clayton and R. Anderson. *The economics of online crime* available at http://www.sfu.ca/iccrc/content/econ.onlinecrime.pdf, last accessed 5 July 2013.

[5] See footnote 4.

[6] See Art. 2, para. 4 on "Security of processing", Citizens Directive 2009/136/EC at http://eur-lex.europa.eu/LexUriServ/LexUriServ.do?uri=OJ:L:2009:337:0011:0036:En:PDF, last accessed December 2011 and Orrick, Data protection alert available at http://www.orrick.com/fileupload/2389.pdf; Outlaw News, Communication providers should log personal data security breaches monthly, Information Commissioner says available at http://www.out-law.com/en/articles/2011/december/communications-providers-should-log-personal-data-security-breaches-monthly-information-commissioner-says/, dated 12 December 2011.

[7] Baker, L.B. and J. Finkle, Sony PlayStation suffers massive data breach available at http://www.reuters.com/article/2011/04/26/us-sony-stoldendata-idUSTRE73P6WB20110426 dated 26 April 2011; Sony data breach: 100 m reasons to beef up security available at http://www.computerweekly.com/news/1280097348/Sony-data-breach-100m-reasons-to-beef-up-security, dated 3 May 2011; Guardian Technology Blog. Sony suffers second data breach with theft of 25m more user details available at http://www.guardian.co.uk/technology/blog/2011/may/03/sony-data-breach-online-entertainment, last accessed 19 December 2011.

Whilst the current data protection framework[8] is currently being updated, it appears that data security breaches are likely to be considered in the forthcoming Data Protection Regulation to extend the reporting of information data security breaches (known as "data security breach notifications") beyond communications providers.

Although the UK data protection framework has been changed to strengthen remedies for individuals and make it mandatory (for communications providers), to notify the UK Information Commissioner, if a data security breach does occur, one of the questions to ask is not so much as enhancing the data protection framework (whilst important), but rather *how* to change the attitudes and mindsets of individuals responsible for data security within their organisations? Other than considering introducing more penalties in the form of criminal sanctions, *education and awareness* within organisations working in tandem with the ICO and for those at a European level with the relevant Data Protection Authority is once again key to this.

In *Harbouring Data: Information security, law and the corporation*,[9] Matwyshyn made the following point (albeit in a US context), which deserves further consideration:

> The biggest challenges in information security frequently involve humans more than they involve technology. Humans, perhaps unlike technology can demonstrate extreme levels of variation in skill and do not always follow logical rules in conduct. They can be emotional actors, driven by perception an emotion as much as by objective reality.[10]

It is not so much as technology in protecting data or limiting access data if humans are not fully aware of the consequences of data breaches. Zetter puts it aptly in a scenario that "I heard many complaints from security professionals about companies. They understood the need to install firewalls and intrusion detection systems but then failed to *monitor* the systems they installed (emphasis added)".[11]

To reinforce her arguments, she gives further examples of information security lapses. A skimming activity involving the thief recording a victim's card and personal ID number was used in a gas station in California.

> Authorities know about the problem, as did the gas station and the banks whose customers were affected but customers did not learn that their cards had been compromised until they discovered fraudulent charges on the cards.[12]

Another example of a data security breach given by the same author involves basic computer standards that were not followed:

> Engineers and computer security experts who grow frustrated by employers who repeatedly ignore warnings about vulnerabilities in a computer system sometimes share information

---

[8] See Chap. 6 on the Data Protection Regulation.

[9] A.M. Matwyshyn (ed.), *Harbouring data: information security, law, and the corporation*, 2009, p. 229.

[10] See footnote 9.

[11] Zetter, K. "Reporting of information security breaches" In: A.M. Matwyshyn (ed.), Harbouring data: information security, law and the corporation, op. cit. n. 16, p. 51.

[12] See footnote 11, at p. 53.

about security problem. Two years ago, I received a tip from an American programmer who helped set up the computer network for a large bank in another country. He told me the bank's website had a major flaw that would allow thieves to install malicious code on a third-party server that allow thieves to serve up a phony bank site to customers to record the account number and password when customers typed them onto a web form. While the bank had taken care to secure its own servers, the programmer explained, it opened its system to a serious vulnerability because it allowed a third party to serve ads to its site. The engineer warned the company several times about the vulnerability, but the warnings fell on deaf ears.[13]

Although the issues tend to focus on human lapses in adopting basic computer security standards which were lacking, it also indicates the difficulty of understanding the nature of the problem and the breadth or scale of the problem and the role played (if any) by the (Data Protection) regulator without recourse to some form of legal remedy (either through data protection laws or specific computer related offences) in the event of a data security breach.

The same author was in support of notification laws in the US states to educate the public about the need for better security on their computers[14] and the need to monitor credit reports and bank accounts whilst the author noted that the main shortcomings in data breach notification laws. Namely, the lack of legal resources for individuals to pursue a data breach claim in the States[15] or the ability of the reporter differentiate between good and bad security when reporting on computer incidents.[16]

From one's perspective, the problem of data security breaches are but a tip of the iceberg, and Data Protection Authorities needs to be engaged not simply in raising awareness amongst those involved with data protection compliance, but also identify how these issues could be dealt with from data security breaches to its remedial stage for the users, whilst engaging organisations to be fully informed of their roles as "data controllers" in how they handle data. For instance, an incentive to encourage organisations to improving data security standards is necessary not simply as a way to conform to the data protection laws but from a consumer perspective. In other words, consumers will lose confidence in the way organisations (public or private) handle their data. How is this shared amongst other organisations with a full degree of transparency (as mandated under the Data Protection Directive transposed within the national data protection laws)? The proposed Data Protection Regulation[17] is likely to highlight and reinforce some of these issues, but whether this can be achieved through compliance rather than the willingness on the part of the organisations to take data security issues seriously is another question.

A further issue is whether national Data Protection Authorities (as in the UK) should take a pre-emptive or proactive rather than a reactive approach to data security breaches.[18]

---

[13] See footnote 11.

[14] See footnote 11, at p. 61.

[15] See footnote 11, at p. 62.

[16] See footnote 11.

[17] See Chap. 6 on the Data Protection Regulation.

[18] See ICO. *Report data breaches or risk tougher sanctions, warns the ICO*, op. cit. n. 12.

In the latest news on data security, the ICO was of the view that it was confounded by the disconnect between staff (in the NHS) awareness on the subject and the number of breaches that occur in the health service [4].

To reinforce the point of data security awareness, Marks and Spencer recently had to contact its customers recently warning them that their email address had been stolen after a US-based email marketing supplier was attacked by a computer hacking incident [5]. According to the FT, Karen Avery, a practice leader for a consultancy firm made the following comment:

> It is essential for a company to map out what information it has, and its economic value, so it can make the right decisions about protecting it. High quality global journalism requires investment. "What a criminal would do is map out the information value chain and look for the weakest link", she says. "Taking this end-to-end approach allows you to understand where the weak links are, and apply the appropriate solutions" [5].

The InfoWorld recently reported a number of data security breaches involving well-known companies such as the PlayStation whereby 77 million customer records were exposed [6], followed by Sony's data security breach resulting in 25 million customer records being exposed [6].

Based on the latest statistics from the ICO on data security breaches,[19] this area of concern is likely to continue with the impending changes to the Data Protection Directive if the proposed Data Protection Regulation is extended to other organisations beyond the electronic communications sector and the mandatory requirement for the appointment of Data Protection officers in organisations.

---

[19] ICO. 1000 data breaches reported to the ICO available at http://www.ico.gov.uk/~/media/documents/pressreleases/2010/1000_DATA_BREACHES280510.ashx, dated 28 May 2010 and ICO: Likely breaches of the DPA received between 6 April 2010 and 22 March 2011, by sector available at http://www.ico.gov.uk/about_us/how_we_comply/disclosure_log/~/media/documents/disclosure_log/IRQ0382403b.ashx, dated 15 April 2011 and ICO Report on the Annual findings of the Information Commissioner's Office, Annual Track, 2011 available at http://www.ico.gov.uk/about_us/research/~/media/documents/library/Corporate/Research_and_reports/annual_track_2011_organisations.ashx, last accessed 9th February 2012 and AlertBoot. UK private sector breaches up 58 % YOY available at http://www.ico.gov.uk/about_us/research/~/media/documents/library/Corporate/Research_and_reports/annual_track_2011_organisations.ashx, dated 9 November 2011.

References

1. Treaty on the European (2011) at http://eur-lex.europa.eu/en/treaties/dat/11992M/htm/11992M. html, Now replaced by the Lisbon Treaty (TFEU) at http://europa.eu/lisbon_treaty/index_ en.htm, Accessed 21 Oct 2011
2. European Commission (2011) Commission's first report on the transposition of the Data Protection Directive at http://ec.europa.eu/justice/policies/privacy/lawreport/report_en.htm. Accessed Dec 2011
3. ICO (2013) Information Security 7 http://www.ico.gov.uk/for_organisations/data_protection/ the_guide/principle_7.aspx. Accessed 4 Jan 2013
4. The Register (2011) ICO: NHS data security breaches are just "plain daft" available at http:// www.theregister.co.uk/2011/10/06/nhs_data_security_breaches/. Accessed 6 Oct 2011
5. Feisted A (2011) "Data security: breaches can result in huge costs" Financial Times, available at http://www.ft.com/cms/s/0/beac7484-04c8-11e1-b309-00144feabdc0.html#axzz1gn1UfhFn. Accessed 8 Nov 2011
6. Leonhard W (2011) "What the latest data security breaches really mean" available at http:// www.infoworld.com/t/data-security/what-the-latest-data-security-breaches-really-mean-239. Accessed 6 Jun 2011

Chapter 3
The Amended Directive on Privacy and Electronic Communications

Abstract This chapter will take a detailed analysis into the amended Directive on Privacy and Electronic Communications, the changes introduced in 2009 and the Data Breach Notification Regulation 611/2013 that was passed in June 2013. The Directive on Privacy and Electronic Communications complements the existing Data Protection Directive and applies data protection rules to public communication providers. This chapter will consider in brief, the notion of "security" under Article 4.2 and what is meant by "personal data breach" within the Directive. This will be further supplemented by an analysis into the Commission Regulation 611/2013 which puts on a legal footing data breach notifications and harmonises data security breach notifications within the EU.

Keywords Directive on privacy and electronic communications • Data security

The Directive on Privacy and Electronic Communications 2002/58/EC ("DPEC") complements the existing Data Protection Directive 95/46/EC by mainly applying the data protection rules to public communications providers. It should be added that originally, DPEC did not cover data security breaches and this measure arose out of concerns after data security lapses involving discs containing users' information that were lost without any satisfactory remedy.[1] As a result, some data protection laws such as UK had to be strengthened to impose heavier penalties for lax security procedures when handling personal information. Furthermore, the ICO identified that the number of discs that were not encrypted was a major problem.[2]

---

[1] BBC.*UK's families put on fraud alert* available at http://news.bbc.co.uk/1/hi/uk_politics/7103566.stm, dated 20 November 2007.

[2] ICO. *Penalty highlights need for encryption of sensitive data* available at http://www.ico.org.uk/news/latest_news/2012/penalty-highlights-need-for-encryption-of-sensitive-data-25102012, dated 25 October 2012.

R. Wong, *Data Security Breaches and Privacy in Europe*, SpringerBriefs in Cybersecurity, DOI: 10.1007/978-1-4471-5586-7_3, © The Author(s) 2013

The DPEC (as amended in 2009) now require that any data security breaches involving providers of public communications should be notified to the national Data Protection Authority.[3]

Before considering the recent Commission Regulation 611/2013 which was passed on 24 June 2013 in detail and makes significant changes to this Directive, below is a short summary of the main provisions to the amended Directive on Privacy and Electronic Communications. This will provide a context before dealing with data security breach notifications in more detail.

Article 4.2 of the DPEC deals with a particular risk of breach of security which requires the providers of publicly available electronic communications network to take appropriate technical and organisational measures to safeguard security of its services. The concept of "security" is quite broad and encompasses protection against accidental or unlawful destruction or accidental loss, attention, unauthorised disclosure or access, in particular where the processing involves the transmission of data over a network and against all other forms of unlawful processing such as wiretapping, possibility of intrusion within the provider's information system to collect all its customers addresses or to manipulate certain data.[4]

Transposition of the Directive by EU Member States is required by 25 May 2011. Article 1(2) of DPEC complements the general Data Protection Directive 95/46/EC. Article 1(3) of the amended DPEC does *not apply* to activities falling outside the scope of the Treaty establishing the EC such as those covered by Titles V and VI of the TEU that are "activities concerning public security, defence, State security (including the economic well-being of the State when the activities relate to State security matters) and the activities of the State in areas of criminal law".[5]

Personal data breach is defined under Article 2(c) as follows:

"Personal data breach" means a breach of security leading to the accidental or unlawful destruction, loss, alteration, unauthorised disclosure of, or access to, personal data transmitted, stored or otherwise processed in connection with the provision of a publicly available electronic communications service in the Community.

This follows the US model of data security breach notifications.[6] Article 4 covers the main provision on the security or processing, requiring that electronic communication service providers take appropriate and organisational measures to safeguard the

---

[3] Article 4(3) Directive 2002/58/EC (amended) which is available at http://ec.europa.eu/justice/data-protection/law/files/recast_20091219_en.pdf), last accessed 9th April 2013.

[4] Poullet, *IT concise law*, p. 165.

[5] Article 1(3) of DPEC.

[6] See NCSL. Security breach notification legislations/laws available athttp://www.ncsl.org/issues-research/telecommunications-information-technology/security-breach-notification-laws.aspx, dated 6 February 2012. See also Romanosky, S. R. Telang and A. Acquisti, "Do data breach disclosure laws reduce identity theft? Journal of Policy Analysis and Management 2011 available at http://papers.ssrn.com/sol3/papers.cfm?abstract_id=1268926, last accessed 9th February 2012; Chandler, J.A. "Negligence liability for breaches of data security" available at http://papers.ssrn.com/sol3/papers.cfm?abstract_id=1268926, dated July 2007; Winn, J.K. "Are "better" security breach notification laws possible? Available at http://papers.ssrn.com/sol3/papers.cfm?abstract_id=1416222, dated 2009.

security of its services if necessary in conjunction with the provider of public communication. Article 4(1)(a) requires that personal data can be accessed only by authorised personnel for legally authorised purposes. Personal data should be protected against any forms of accidental or unlawful destruction, accidental loss or alteration and that security policies should be implemented to protect personal data. The involvement of Data Protection Authorities in auditing data to assess their security breaches is clearly provided under the DPEC. The responsibility lies with the service provider of publicly available communications to inform users of any data security breaches that may occur. There are very extensive changes made to DPEC. Article 4(3) also further requires users to be informed by service providers of any breach without any delay if it was likely to adversely affect the privacy of the individual. However, there is no need to notify where the authority such as the UK ICO had been informed that appropriate measures were taken to deal with security breaches.[7]

Article 4(4) requires the relevant authority, the UK ICO for instance to adopt guidelines and where necessary issue instructions concerning the circumstances in which providers should notify about personal data security breaches. The format and delivery of these instructions are fairly detailed within the DPEC. For instance, an inventory should be provided for any personal data breach and any steps to remedy the breach.

Article 4(5) confer powers of the Commission in conjunction with ENISA, Article 29 Working Party and the European Data Protection Supervisor to adopt technical implementing measures on the circumstances found and procedures appropriate to the information and notification requirements referred to within the same provision.

Article 5(1) deals with the confidentiality of communications by public communication providers whereby the consent of the subscriber is required except where authorised to do so in accordance with Article 15(1).[8]

Article 5(3) requires that "Member States shall ensure that the storing of information or the gaining of access to information already stored in the terminal equipment of a subscriber or user is only allowed on condition that the subscriber or user concerned has given his or her consent…having been provided with clear and comprehensive information in accordance with Directive 95/46/EC, *inter alia* about the purposes of the processing of personal data".

---

[7] Article 4(3) of DPEC provides that 'Notification of a personal data breach to a subscriber or individual concerned shall not be required if the provider has demonstrated to the satisfaction of the competent authority that it has implemented appropriate technological protection measures, and that those measures were applied to the data concerned by the security breach. Such technological protection measures shall render the data unintelligible to any person who is not authorised to access it'.

[8] Article 15(1) of DPEC provides that "Member States may adopt legislative measures to restrict the scope of the rights and obligations provided for in Article 5, Article 6, Article 8(1), (2), (3) and (4) and Article 9 of this Directive when such restriction constitutes a necessary, appropriate and proportionate measure within a democratic society to safeguard national security (i.e. State security), defence, public security and the prevention, investigation, detection and prosecution of criminal offences or of unauthorised use of the electronic communication system, as referred to in Article 13(1) of Directive 95/46/EC."

The other changes include the definition of location data to mean:

> Any data processed in an electronic communications network or by an electronic communications service, indicating the geographic position of the terminal equipment of a user of a publicly available electronic communications service.

More importantly, Article 5(3) of the DPEC is now replaced so that the express consent of users is required before cookies could be installed:

> Member States shall ensure that the storing of information, or the gaining of access to information already stored, in the terminal equipment of a subscriber or user is only allowed on condition that the subscriber or user concerned has *given his or her consent*, having been provided with clear and comprehensive information, in accordance with Directive 95/46/EC, inter alia, about the purposes of the processing. This shall not prevent any technical storage or access for the sole purpose of carrying out the transmission of a communication over an electronic communications network, or as strictly necessary in order for the provider of an information society service explicitly requested by the subscriber or user to provide the service (emphasis added).

This has been the subject of much discussion particularly over the practical realities of asking user's permission before putting a cookie on the PC and came into force in the UK on May 2011.[9] Previously, the DPEC required that users be informed before any cookies of this nature were installed. However, the change represents a shift from being informed to obtaining an opt-in express consent and would have an impact on those that use cookies to track users or build online profiles of their users (this practice is known as "behavioural advertising[10]"). At present, the UK ICO has changed its view so that implied consent will suffice to have cookies on their PC.[11] This recognises the practical problems and opposition by business how this is likely to work in practice and the inconvenience of accessing websites without users enabling cookie access.

Under Article 6, the traffic data of subscribers and users of public communications remains largely unchanged from the former Directive.

Location data showing the location or whereabouts of the individual is still covered under Article 9 with exceptions to identification covered under Arts. 10 (malicious or nuisance calls; emergency calls) and 13 (spam mail). What remains increasingly

---

[9] BBC. *Thousands of websites in breach of new cookie law* available at http://www.bbc.co.uk/news/technology-18206810, dated 26 May 2012. Arthur, C. *Cookies law changed at the 11th h to introduce implied consent* available at http://www.guardian.co.uk/technology/2012/may/26/cookies-law-changed-implied-consent, dated 26th May 2012.

[10] Steel, E. and J. Angwin. *On the web's cutting edge, anonymity in name only* available at http://online.wsj.com/article/SB10001424052748703294904575385532109190198.html?mod=googlenews_wsj, dated 3 August 2010 and Article 29 Working Party. Opinion 2/2010 on online behavioural advertising available at http://ec.europa.eu/justice/policies/privacy/docs/wpdocs/2010/wp171_en.pdf, dated 22 June 2010; Hirsch, D. The law and policy of online privacy: regulation, self-regulation or co-regulation? Available at http://works.bepress.com/dennis_hirsch/1/, last accessed 16th April 2013.

[11] Outlaw. *ICO to change cookie policy to recognise implied consent* available at http://www.out-law.com/en/articles/2013/january/ico-to-change-cookie-policy-to-recognise-implied-consent/, dated 28th January 2013.

uncertain is whether location data is likely to be a pervasive issue with the rise of smartphones. Applications on smartphones that enable user's location to be identified such as googlemaps or location of user on twitter or gaming applications means that consent once given for a specific purpose maybe difficult to withdraw if such services becomes imperative such as finding a specific location. It is also becoming possible for individuals to track other individuals through the use of smartphones meaning anonymising location of an individual's whereabouts may not also be possible.[12] In the context of cybersecurity, the location of a miscreant or criminal may be useful to law enforcement authorities if a search order was placed or alternatively, a spouse tracking their other spouse or employers tracking their employees. The list could go on, but indicates how sensitive such information would be, if taken in a specific context.

On the whole, the amended Directive has been to clarify the provisions and strengthen the rights of individuals in the context of public communications.

The UK has implemented the Directive through the Privacy and Electronic Communications (EC Directive) (Amendment) Regulations 2011.[13] There is specific guidance on cookies and whether consent can be implied.[14] It should be emphasised that the amendments to the Directive on Privacy and Electronic Communications are not simply aimed at cookies but is much broader to cover data security breach notifications whilst most of the other provisions such as traffic data and location data stands.

3.1 Commission Regulation 611/2013

As mentioned earlier, the Commission Regulation 611/2013[15] was passed recently to deal with the notification of personal data breaches under Directive 2002/58/EC. It comes into force on 25 August 2013 and is binding on all EU Member States (Article 288 TFEU). No further implementation is needed.

According to recital 5 and Article 1, the Regulation is *only* limited to the notification of personal data breaches by providers of publicly available electronic communications services.

---

[12] *Geolocation tagging in smart-phones to potentially cause major security risks* available at http://www.eetimes.com/electronics-news/4233719/Geo-location-tagging-in-smartphones-to-potentially-cause-major-security-risks, dated 1 January 2012. Napley, K. *Smartphones and geolocation data* available at http://www.lexology.com/library/detail.aspx?g=d15b1b10-8125-4d5c-aa52-07265d3560a0, dated 20 October 2011.

[13] SI 2011/1208.

[14] ICO. New EU cookie law available at http://www.ico.org.uk/for_organisations/privacy_and_electronic_communications/the_guide/cookies, last accessed 16th April 2013.

[15] Commission Regulation (EU) No. 611/2013 of 24 June 2013 on the measures applicable to the notification of personal data breaches under Directive 2002/58/EC of the European Parliament and of the Council on privacy and electronic communications, OJ L173/2, dated 26 June 2013.

It does not set out in detail the technical implementing measures on Article 4(2) of Directive 2002/58/EC on informing the subscribers where a particular risk of a breach of the security of the network was concerned (recital 5) and follows from Article 4(3)(1) of Directive 2002/58/EC that providers should notify to the competent national authority all personal data breaches (recital 6 and Article 2).

The provider should notify personal data breaches to the competent national authority no later than 24 h following the detection of the personal data breach where feasible (Article 2(1) and (1)). Detection of a personal data breach is deemed to have taken place if the provider has acquired sufficient awareness that a security incident has occurred leading to the compromisation of personal data (Article 3(2)).

If the provider does not have all the information required under Annex 1 (identification of the provider; further information on the personal data breach or possible additional notification or individuals concerned or possible cross border issues), then the provider would make an initial notification within the 24 h period and a second notification as soon as possible and no later than 3 days and contain the information set out in section 2 of Annex 1 of the Regulation (Article 2(3)). Should the provider be unable to provide all the information within this timeframe, the provider should provide as much information as possible within that timeframe and an explanation for the delay of the remaining information required to the competent national authority (Article 2(3)).

The competent national authority is required to provide a secure electronic means for the notification of personal data breaches and information on the procedures for its access and use (Article 2(4)). The type of format could be based on XML (recital 11) and contain the information provided under Annex I in the relevant languages to enable the provider to comply with a similar notification procedure (recital 11).

Article 2(5) provides that where the personal data breach affects subscribers or individuals from other Member States other than that of the competent national authority in which the personal data breach occurs, the competent national authority would be required to inform the other national authorities concerned. The Commission would have to create and maintain a list of competent national authorities and the appropriate contact points (Article 2(5)).

Article 3 deals with the notification of the security breach to the subscriber or individual. According to Article 3(1), where the personal data breach is likely to adversely affect the personal data or privacy of a subscriber or individual, the provider should notify the subscriber or individual as well as the provider. Article 3(2) provides the following circumstances to be taken into account when assessing whether a personal data would adversely affect the personal data or privacy of a subscriber or individual. This would be the nature and content of the personal data concerned where the data concerns financial information, special categories of data referred in Article 8(1) of the Data Protection Directive (such as health, trade union membership etc.); location data (whereabouts of an individual), Internet log files, web browsing histories, e-mail data and itemised call lists (Article 3(2)(a)). The likely consequences resulting from personal data breach would include identity theft, fraud, physical harm, psychological distress, humiliation or damage to reputation and circumstances where the data was stolen or when the provider knows that the data was in possession of an unauthorised third party (Article 3(2) (b) and (c)).

Informing the subscriber or individual should be done as soon as possible without any undue delay and provided in a clear and understandable language following the identification of persona data breach as set out in Article 2(2) (Articles 3(3) and 3(4)). The notification of the subscriber or individual is entirely separate from the notification to the national authority.

It is possible for the provider to delay the notification to the subscriber or individual if it may put at the risk the proper investigation of the personal data breach such as criminal investigation or other personal data breaches and agreement should be reach with the competent national authority on the delay until the competent national authority considers it possible to notify the personal data breach (Article 3(5) and recital 13).

Advertisements of personal data breaches that have occurred in major national or local newspapers maybe necessary if the provider is unable to identify within the timeframe as required under Article 3(3)). Annex II of the Regulation requires that the advertisement provides an itemised of what should be included such as summary of the incident, and nature and content of the incident and likely consequences resulting from the breach.

According to Article 3(6), the form of communication by the provider to the subscriber or individual should ensure the prompt receipt of information and are appropriately secured according to the state of art.

Article 4(1) of the Regulation, however, provides that it is not necessary to notify the data security breach if the provider can show that it has implemented appropriate technological protection measures such that it renders the data unintelligible to any person not authorised to access this. For instance, the data was encrypted before the data was lost. Article 4(2) develops this by considering that data has encrypted with a standardised algorithm, the key used to decrypt the data was not compromised in any security breach and the key used to encrypt the data was generated so that it could not be ascertained by available technological means by anyone who was not authorised to have access to the key. The other circumstance would be where the data was replaced by its hashed value calculated with a standardised cryptographic keyed hash function and the key was not compromised.

Article 4(3) provides that the Commission could in consultation with other competent national authorities through the Article 29 Working Party, the ENISA, the European Data Protection Supervisor publish an indicative list of appropriate technological measures according to current practices referred to under Article 4(1).

Article 5 provides that if another provider is contracted to deliver part of the electronic communications service without having a direct contractual relationship, the other provider should notify the contracting provider immediately where a personal data breach had occurred.

Article 6 of the Regulation provides that within 3 years of the entry of the Regulation, the Commission should provide a report on the application of the Regulation, its effectiveness and its impact on providers, subscribers and individuals. This review should be linked where possible to any review of Directive 2002/58/EC (recital 21). This could contain statistics provided by the national competent authorities of the personal data breaches that were notified, the number of personal data breaches notified to the competent national authority, the number of personal data breaches notified and so on (recital 22).

Although the Regulation will harmonise the procedures for the reporting of data security breaches, some Member States such as the UK have already data breach notification procedures in place,[16] but the regulation will reinforce the need for transparency and put on a legal footing the notification of data security breaches.

Hand in hand with this Directive and Data Breach Notification Regulation is the forthcoming Data Protection Regulation,[17] which is likely to replace the Data Protection Directive 95/46/EC and a specific Directive dealing with data protection in the context of law enforcement. This is considered in Chap. 6.

What follows is a discussion of the issues (from the perspective of information security) by the Article 29 Working Party and the European Commission leading up to the proposed Data Protection Regulation.

---

[16] See UK ICO. Guidance on data security breach management available at http://www.ico.org.uk/~/media/documents/library/Data_Protection/Practical_application/guidance_on_data_security_breach_management.ashx, last accessed 19 August 2013.

[17] Data Protection Regulation is available at http://ec.europa.eu/justice/data-protection/document/review2012/com_2012_11_en.pdf, dated 25 January 2012. For further reading into the background developments preceding the Data Protection Regulation, see Wong, R. "The future of privacy" (2011) CLSR 27(1) 53-57 and Wong, R. "Data Protection: idealisms and realisms" (SSRN) available at http://papers.ssrn.com/sol3/papers.cfm?abstract_id=1985298, last accessed 29 March 2012.

Chapter 4
Article 29 Working Party: Future of Privacy

Abstract This chapter reviews the recent opinion by the Article 29 Working Party on the *Future of Privacy*. In particular, the role that privacy enhancing technologies (often known as "PETS") play in the context of information security and the accountability principle on which security breach notifications is based that will be introduced in the forthcoming Data Protection Regulation.

Keywords Article 29 working party • Future of privacy

In 2009, the Article 29 Working Party published a recent opinion on the *Future of Privacy*.[1] The emphasis was mainly on privacy enhancing technologies ("PETS") in the context of biometrics and video surveillance. Data minimisation; user-friendly systems and data confidentiality were some of the issues mentioned in this Opinion to reinforce the need to for more privacy protection.

Other than emphasising data protection as a fundamental right, the Opinion was a joint view of the Article 29 Working Party and the Working Party on Police and Justice in response to the Commission's consultation on the legal framework for the fundamental right to protection of personal data.

The aim in this section is therefore, not to revisit the main recommendations arising from this Opinion, but to focus on the salient points dealing with information security in the context of Cyber security. Therefore, this section will consider in brief, privacy enhancing technologies and the accountability principle.

---

[1] See Art. 29 Working Party. "The future of privacy", WP 168, at http://ec.europa.eu/justice/policies/privacy/docs/wpdocs/2009/wp168_en.pdf, adopted 1 December 2011; Wong, R. "Data Protection: the future of privacy", (2011) 27(1) CLSR 53–57. More details can be found in recital 110 of the proposed Data Protection Regulation available at http://ec.europa.eu/justice/newsroom/data-protection/news/120125_en.htm, dated 25 January 2012. These proposals are still tentative subject to approval at EU level and *European Commission proposes a comprehensive reform of the data protection rules* available at http://ec.europa.eu/justice/newsroom/data-protection/news/120125_en.htm, dated 25 January 2012.

R. Wong, *Data Security Breaches and Privacy in Europe*, SpringerBriefs in Cybersecurity, 17
DOI: 10.1007/978-1-4471-5586-7_4, © The Author(s) 2013

4.1 Privacy Enhancing Technologies

"Privacy enhancing technologies" is a term to refer specifically to the minimisation of the use of personal information either through anonymisation or pseudonymisation either online or offline.[2] In the context of information security, it principally deals with collecting little personal information from its users by anonymising or pseudonymising personal data. Whilst not a new concept, PETS has received support from the European Commission as early as 2003.[3] In the Opinion, the main basis for PETs stems from Article 17 of the DPD which required organisations in their role as data controllers to implement appropriate technical and organisational measures. According to the same Opinion,[4] PETS, in practice, have not been used to ensure that privacy is embedded in ICT. Services and technology should, according to the Opinion, be designed with privacy by default settings.[5]

The Article 29 WP was of the view that privacy by design principle should be binding on technology designers and producers as well as data controllers who have to decide upon the acquisition and use of ICTs and the recent German case which reached the German Constitutional Court created a constitutional right in the confidentiality and integrity of information technology system.[6] Whilst this was a decision from the German courts, it is likely to have implications upon organisations operating within Germany or process data belonging to German citizens by requiring them to respect the confidentiality rules on their PCs. The decision opens debate about the need for information systems to be robust. The legal ruling reinforces the need for data controllers to understand and grasp the implications arising from deficient security procedures resulting in security lapses and loss of personal information.

Literature dealing specifically with Privacy Enhancing Technologies has tended to focus on specific disciplines such as computer science or sociological standpoint.

A glance at the UK ICO's recent guidance in 2008 indicates some views on embracing privacy enhancing technologies.[7]

---

[2] Europa, Privacy Enhancing Technologies (PETs) available at http://europa.eu/rapid/press-release_MEMO-07-159_en.htm, dated 2 May 2007.

[3] See European Commission. *First report on the implementation of the Data Protection Directive* at para. 4.3 available at http://eur-lex.europa.eu/LexUriServ/site/en/com/2003/com 2003_0265en01.pdf, dated 15 May 2003.

[4] Art. 29 Working Party Opinion., op. cit. n. 31 at para. 45.

[5] See footnote 4.

[6] Abel, W. and B. Schafer. *The German Constitutional Court on the Right in Confidentiality and Integrity of Information Technology Systems—a case report on BVerfG, NJW 2008, 822* (2009) 6:1*SCRIPTed*106, http://www.law.ed.ac.uk/ahrc/script-ed/vol6-1/abel.asp.

[7] ICO. *Privacy by design: an overview of privacy enhancing technologies*, available at http://www.ico.org.uk/for_organisations/data_protection/topic_guides/~/media/documents/pdb_report_html/PBD_PETS_PAPER.ashx, dated 26th November 2008 and ICO, Privacy by design available at http://www.ico.org.uk/news/current_topics/privacy_by_design_conference, last accessed 9th April 2013.

Although a slow moving field in research, it is likely to be brought into much sharper focus when the proposed changes are considered under the Data Protection Regulation. This will be considered in Chap. 6.

Some of the examples, whereby the privacy by design principle[8] could be applied include biometric identifiers which should be under the control of the data subject; video surveillance in public transportation systems or patient names and other personal identifiers in hospitals' information systems.

Specific legislation may be required for certain sectors. For example, RFID technology, social networks, behavioural advertisements involve the collection of personal information.[9]

In the latest version (unauthorised) that was released on a proposed Regulation,[10] there is mention in Articles 20 and 27(3) of Privacy by Design principles with Article 20 of the Proposed Regulation setting out the main the duties for data controllers in the context of data protection by default.

> 1. Having regard to the *state of the art and the cost of implementation*, the *controller* shall, both at the time of the determination of the means for processing and at the time of the processing itself, implement appropriate technical and organisational measures and procedures in such a way that the processing will meet the requirements of this Regulation and ensure the protection of the rights of the data subject.
> 2. The *controller* shall implement mechanisms for ensuring that, by default, only those personal data are processed which are necessary for each specific purpose of the processing and are especially not be collected or retained beyond the minimum necessary for those purposes, both in terms of the amount of the data and the time of their storage. In particular, those mechanisms shall ensure that by default personal data are not made *accessible to an indefinite number* of individuals (emphasis added).[11]

The provision on PETs is not surprising in light of the recent discussions by the Article 29 Working Party and the European Commission in dealing with changes to the Data Protection Directive.

It should be added that in the latest paper entitled *Online privacy: towards informational self-determination on the internet*,[12] the authors took the view that there has been a lack of *incentive* for enterprises to design privacy enhancing products. The proposed regulation is likely to remedy and provide more support in this area.[13] To give an example, PETS have been slow to make its way to the statute books and

---

[8] See footnote 7, at para. 52.

[9] See footnote 7, at para. 56.

[10] European Commission. Proposal for a European Regulation available at http://statewatch.org/news/2011/dec/eu-com-draft-dp-reg-inter-service-consultation.pdf, last accessed 4th January 2013.

[11] See footnote 10.

[12] Krontiris, I. *Online privacy: towards informational self-determination on the internet* available at http://www.dagstuhl.de/en/program/calendar/semhp/?semnr=11061, dated February 2011.

[13] For an in-depth study, see LSE. *Study on the economic benefits of PETS, final report to the European Commission,* available at http://ec.europa.eu/justice/policies/privacy/docs/studies/final_report_pets_16_07_10_en.pdf, dated July 2010.

according to one expert, PETS found their way in federal privacy laws (German Federal Data Protection Law, the *Bundesdatenschutzgesetz*) as well as in most German Länder laws (such as Articles 5 and 6 of the *LDSG Schleswig–Holstein*).[14] PETs are not mentioned under the *UK Data Protection Act 1998* (DPA 1998), but this could simply be explained by reference to the fact that the UK DPA 1998 implements the Data Protection Directive 95/46/EC which predates internet era developments. The only point to add is that the seventh data protection principle under Sch. 1 of the UK Data Protection Act 1998 refers to technical and security organisational measures to be made which is the closest to any discussion on PETS (if any).

4.2 Accountability Principle

The accountability principle was recommended in the Opinion[15] as one measure to be introduced in changes to the Data Protection Directive, which would make data controllers responsible for carrying out the necessary measures and ensure that substantive principles and obligations of the current Directive were followed.

Yet the Opinion was of the view that more proactive or reactive measures could be adopted to support the accountability principle such as security breach notifications[16] and the reinforcement of enforcement powers of Data Protection Authorities. This would further strengthen the aims of the Data Protection Directive.

The latest Data Protection Regulation proposals specifically make reference to the accountability principle. Under Article 13 of the Data Protection Regulation, for instance, in relation to recipients, data controllers shall "commence any rectification or erasure carried out in accordance with Articles 16 and 17 to each recipient to whom the data have been disclosed, unless this proves impossible or involves a disproportionate effort." Furthermore, Article 14(6) also requires data controllers to provide appropriate measures to protect the data subject's legitimate interests.

What it does not deal with is the outsourcing of data to third parties and whether they could ensure data security. Consider examples of cloud computing[17]

---

[14] See footnote 13.

[15] Op. cit. n. 31.

[16] Op. cit. n. 31 at p. 21.

[17] A good starting point into the discussion on cloud computing is a collection of essays in S. Gutwirth (ed.) (et al.). *Computers, privacy and data protection: an element of choice,* 2011, pp. 345–457. See also ENISA, *Cloud computing risk assessment,* dated 20 November 2009 available at http://www.enisa.europa.eu/act/rm/files/deliverables/cloud-computing-risk-assessment and NIST definition of cloud computing at http://csrc.nist.gov/publications/nistpubs/800-145/SP800-145.pdf, dated September 2011 and NIST, *Final version of NIST cloud computing definition published,* dated 25 October 2011 available at http://www.nist.gov/itl/csd/cloud-102511.cfm. W.K. Hon, C. Millard and I. Walden 'Who is responsible for "Personal Data" in Cloud Computing' available at http://papers.ssrn.com/sol3/papers.cfm?abstract_id=1783577 and W.K. Hon, C. Millard and I. Walden 'Who is responsible for "Personal Data" in Cloud Computing?, Part 2', available at http://papers.ssrn.com/sol3/papers.cfm?abstract_id=1794130.

where data (whether it includes personal information or not) is uploaded onto the "cloud"? Is data encrypted? Some of these issues have been addressed in the proposed Regulation. Similarly, issues such as social networking providers are also likely to bring challenges and again, this is addressed in the proposed Data Protection Regulation.

Chapter 5
European Commission Communication Opinion 2010

Abstract This chapter will consider a brief introduction to the European Commission Communication Opinion which was published in 2010. The European Commission sets out its aim when reviewing the changes to the Data Protection Directive in its "Comprehensive approach on personal data protection in the European Union". It should be considered in brief in the context of "information security" since there are several issues that the Opinion considers. It will provide a backdrop to the forthcoming Data Protection Regulation.

Keywords European commission communication opinion • Information security

Published in 2010, the European Commission sets out its aim when reviewing the changes to the Data Protection Directive in its "Comprehensive approach on personal data protection in the European Union". It should be considered in brief in the context of "information security" since there are several issues that the Opinion considers. It covers, *inter alia*, the ability of an individual to control his or her data ("individualistic" right). According to the European Commission, for individuals to enjoy a high level of data protection[1] two preconditions were necessary. Namely, the limitation of the data controller's processing in relation to its purposes ("data minimization principle") and the retention by data subjects of an effective control over their own data. The European Commission notes that the right to access the data is already provided under the existing framework. However, the main drawback is that the exercise of these rights is not harmonised in most Member States. According to the European Commission, it should therefore be clarified and strengthened. This could be achieved by first, strengthening the principle of data minimization; improving the modalities for the actual

---

[1] European Commission. Communication from the Commission to the European Parliament, the Council, the Economic and Social Committee and the Committee of the Regions: A comprehensive approach on personal data in the European Union, COM (2010) 609 final, p. 7.

R. Wong, *Data Security Breaches and Privacy in Europe*, SpringerBriefs in Cybersecurity, 23
DOI: 10.1007/978-1-4471-5586-7_5, © The Author(s) 2013

exercise of the rights of access, rectification, erasure or blocking of data; ensuring free and informed consent; protecting sensitive data and making remedies and sanctions more effective.

In the context of information security, the strengthening of the data subject's rights can be limited if a data security breach were to occur. For instance, a bank may lose data of its customers. Or the user may not realize that his data was being gathered through the number of clicks of websites that he or she visits.[2] Similarly, if search terms inputted on the Google search engine[3] could be easily traced back to the user or recorded by the search engine,[4] it is fair to argue that the strengthening of the individual's rights are limited because he or she loses the control of their data when placed in the hands of third parties. How can data security be assured? It will be seen that the proposed Regulation is likely to impose heavier penalties for data controllers who have lax security breaches under Article 79 which will be considered in more detail in Chap. 6.

The European Commission also considered the issue of data controller's responsibility by making the appointment of an independent data protection office mandatory[5] and harmonising the rules related to their tasks and competences including an obligation for data controller to carry out a data protection impact in specific cases such as when sensitive data are being processed or when the type of processing otherwise involves specific risks.[6] This will be significant since such an obligation *does not* currently arise, nor does it deal with the person responsible for data security within an organisation or who would notify the Data Protection Authority in the event of a data security lapse.

---

[2] See Wong, R. and D.B. Garrie, Demystifying clickstream data: a European and US perspective, *Emory International Law Review 20*(2) 563–589 (2006); Skok, G. Establishing a legitimate expectation of privacy in clickstream data, 6 Mich. Telecomm. Tech. L. Rev. 61 (2000) available at http://www.mttlr.org/volsix/skok.html; Kovarsky, L. Tolls on the Information Superhighway: Entitlement Defaults for clickstream data, *Virginia Law Review* 89, 1037–1104 (2003).

[3] Barbaro, M. *A face is exposed for AOL searcher no. 4417749* available at http://select.nytimes.com/gst/abstract.html?res=F10612FC345B0C7A8CDDA10894DE404482, dated 9 August 2006. See also ENISA. *How to strengthen the EU legislation, improve international cooperation and secure the growing market of internet services. Position paper presented to the LIBE Committee of the European Parliament at the public hearing entitled "Data Protection and Search Engines on Internet (eg: the Google-DoubleClick case)"*, dated January 2008.

[4] See footnote 3.

[5] Under the proposed Data Protection Regulation, Articles 35–37 lays down the duties required for data protection officers. It would be a requirement for organisations employing over 250 employees.

[6] Articles 33 and 34 of the proposed Data Protection Regulation deals with the impact of assessment data. Article 39 of the Regulation also provides details on certification mechanism and data protection seals.

Chapter 6
Proposed Data Protection Regulation 2012: Data Security Breach Notifications

Abstract This chapter will consider the proposed Data Protection Regulation introduced in January 2012 and in particular, data breach notifications under Articles 32 and 32. Under Article 31, there would be a duty to notify data breaches within 24 h to the Data Protection Authority, but the time frame is still under consideration by the European Parliament. The nature and form of data security breaches will also be considered under the Data Protection Regulation.

Keywords Data Protection Regulation • Data security breach notifications

Introduced in January 2012, the main provision dealing with data security breach notifications is covered under Articles 31 and 32. It should be added that the current Data Protection Directive 95/46/EC *does not* have a specific provision dealing with data breaches so there is no obligation for the data controller to notify the Data Protection Authority.

However, as alluded to earlier, data breaches tend to be investigated by the Data Protection Authority if they know of such data breach incidents particularly where this is highly publicised as with the example of Sony.

Under Article 31 of the proposed Data Protection Regulation, there is a duty to notify data breaches within 24 h to the Data Protection Authorities.

Danagher argues that the time limit for notification is too short and that it imposes a significant burden on data controllers.[1]

The question arises is what types of data loss should be reported to the Data Protection Authority? Who should notify data breach and in what way should this be provided? What about data loss involving employees or customers? Are these incidents similar to loss of data involving a mobile phone containing contact

---

[1] Danagher, L. "An assessment of the Data Protection Regulation: does it effectively protect data"? available at http://ejlt.org//article/view/171, *European Journal of Law and Technology*, 3(3) last accessed 23rd February 2013.

R. Wong, *Data Security Breaches and Privacy in Europe*, SpringerBriefs in Cybersecurity, DOI: 10.1007/978-1-4471-5586-7_6, © The Author(s) 2013

details or laptop which was not password protected or encrypted? What about if the laptop was stolen?

According to Article 4(9) of the Data Protection Regulation, a "personal data breach" is defined as a "breach of security leading to the accidental or unlawful destruction, loss, alteration, unauthorized disclosure of, or access to, personal data transmitted, stored or otherwise processed".

This definition is fairly broad and would cover the above example given. The Data Protection Regulation places the onus on the data controller to show that it has complied with the data protection laws.[2]

The ICO has recently published its response to data breach notifications, taking the view that the timescale is not realistic.[3] It may also be the case that the data subject maybe informed before or at the same time as the Data Protection Authority. The ICO further added that some element of risk will need to be introduced.[4] Some breaches will be more consequential than others. Furthermore, the ICO was clear to point out that data breach notifications under the Regulation should be consistent with data breach notifications under the UK Privacy and Electronic Communications Regulations (that implement DPEC).[5]

The ICO further expressed reservations over the two step notification scheme recommended by the Article 29 Working Party which would involve notification within 24 h and more detailed notification within 3 days later.

The ICO further noted whether 3 days was long enough? Large electronic communication providers may need more time to conduct and complete investigations into data security breaches. The ICO was particularly concerned about the need to have a coherent approach and avoid a dual notification system from two separate legislations, DPEC and the Data Protection Regulation.

In terms of communicating the breach to the data subject, this should be done without any undue delay. However, it was further noted that there would be differences if the data that was lost was encrypted. In this case, the ICO was of the view that there would be no data breach because only encrypted data was lost.

To give a hypothetical example, if a bank loses customers information which contained their name and address and bank account, then it would be required to notify the data subject. If, however, it had lost the information, but it was in encrypted form, there would be no need to notify as the data was still encrypted.

---

[2] Article 5(1)(f) of the proposed Data Protection Regulation available at http://ec.europa.eu/justice/data-protection/document/review2012/com_2012_11_en.pdf, last accessed 17th April 2013.

[3] ICO. *Proposed new EU General Data Protection Regulation: article by article analysis paper* available at http://www.ico.gov.uk/news/~/media/documents/library/Data_Protection/Research_and_reports/ico_proposed_dp_regulation_analysis_paper_20130212_pdf.ashx, dated 12 February 2013.

[4] Ibid., at pp. 3–4.

[5] Ibid., at p. 40 (Article 32 DP Regulation).

Similarly, if a social networking site had been hacked compromising users' profile, then they would have to notify of this breach. If however, this was in encrypted form, it would be unlikely to require a data security breach notification.

The ICO highlighted the number of incidents involving data security breaches involving encrypted data in 2012 and took the view that encrypting data was not difficult and that data controllers needed to be careful in the way they protect data.[6]

At the time of writing, the European Parliament[7] had made amendments to the Regulation by extending the time for notification to 3 days.[8] The Data Protection Authority will be obliged to keep a register of the data breach notifications. To prevent notification fatigue, only data breaches that were is likely to adversely affect the protection of the personal data or privacy of the data subject, for example in cases of identity theft or fraud, financial loss, physical harm, significant humiliation or damage to reputation would be notified to the data subject (amended Article 32). The notification would include a description of the nature of the personal data breach and information regarding the rights, including possibilities on redress. In this instance, data subjects would know what their remedial rights are following a data security breach. Failure to notify the Data Protection Authority or the data subject of a breach would result in a fine that does not exceed 1,000,000 EUR or 2 % of the annual turnover for an enterprise (amended Article 79(6)) that intentionally or negligently infringes the provision of the Regulation.[9]

According to recital 67 of the Regulation, the European Parliament proposes to extend data breach notifications within 3 days.

A personal data breach may, if not addressed in an adequate and timely manner, result in substantial economic loss and social harm, including identity fraud, to the individual concerned. Therefore, as soon as the controller becomes aware that such a breach has occurred, the controller should notify the breach to the supervisory authority without undue delay and, where feasible, within 72 h. Where this cannot achieved within *72 h*, an explanation of the reasons for the delay should accompany the notification. The individuals whose personal data could be adversely affected by the breach should be notified without undue delay in order to allow them to take the necessary precautions. A breach should be considered as adversely *affecting the personal data or privacy of a data subject where it could result in, for example, identity theft or fraud, physical harm, significant humiliation or damage to reputation.* The notification should describe the nature of the personal data breach as well as recommendations as well as recommendations for the individual concerned to mitigate potential adverse effects. Notifications to data subjects should be made as soon as reasonably feasible, and in close cooperation with the supervisory

---

[6] ICO. *Our approach to encryption* available at http://www.ico.org.uk/news/current_topics/Our_approach_to_encryption, last accessed 16th April 2013.

[7] See European Parliament, *Draft report* 2012/11 available at http://www.europarl.europa.eu/meetdocs/2009_2014/documents/libe/pr/922/922387/922387en.pdf and http://www.europarl.europa.eu/oeil/popups/ficheprocedure.do?reference=2012/0011(COD), last accessed 23rd February 2013.

[8] Ibid.

[9] Ibid.

authority and respecting guidance provided by it or other relevant authorities (e.g. law enforcement authorities) (emphasis added).[10]

According to the report, the European Parliament also welcomed the proposed shift from notification requirements to the Data Protection Authorities (DPAs) to practical accountability and corporate Data Protection Officers (DPOs).

Finally, in a separate development a regulation[11] would be introduced to supplement the Directive on Privacy and Electronic Communications. This specifically provides that data breaches should be notified within 24 h (Article 2) with the possibility of extending this to 3 days (Article 2(3)). Article 2(5) provides that the relevant competent national authority would be required to inform other national authorities where the data breach affects individuals from other Member States. This is likely to be more applicable to multinational companies or large organisations who process large amounts of data involving individuals. Article 3 places an obligation on the ISP or electronic communications provider to notify individuals if their personal data has been compromised.[12] A list of factors to assess how an individual's adverse circumstances are affected is provided under Article 3(2) of the Regulation. There is no obligation to notify the individual or user if the ISP or telecommunication provider can show that it has adopted technological measures to the Data Protection Authority (Article 4). For instance, data was encrypted before it was lost (Article 4(2)). According to one practitioner, "there is a risk that telecos encryption methods which do not appear on the approved list may have difficulty in demonstrating to the regulator that the breached data have been rendered sufficiently unintelligible to third parties. This would leave telcos in an uncertain position and pressure them to change their current security measures to those approved".[13]

---

[10] Recital 67, Proposed Data Protection Regulation available at http://www.europarl.europa. eu/meetdocs/2009_2014/documents/libe/pr/922/922387/922387en.pdf, last accessed 23rd February 2013. At the time of writing, the Commission was of the view that if the Telecom and ISP operators have adhered to their guidelines, they would not have to inform users of a data breach. *See EU citizens to remain in the dark on data breaches* available at http://euobserver.com/justice/120622 and *New data breach rules for EU telecoms companies can be viewed as test of data protection proposals says expert* http://www.out-law.com/en/articles/2013/june/new-data-breach-rules-for-eu-telecoms-companies-can-be-viewed-as-test-of-data-protection-proposals-says-expert/, dated 25 June 2013 and Heath, N. *Data breaches: Telcos and ISPs have 24 hoiurs to come clean, says* http://www.zdnet.com/data-breaches-telcos-and-isps-have-24-hours-to-come-clean-says-eu-7000017217/, dated 24 June 2013.

[11] Proposed Commision Regulation on the measures applicable to the notification of personal data breaches under Directive 2002/58/EC on privacy and electronic communications at http://ec. europa.eu/information_society/newsroom/cf/dae/document.cfm?action=display&doc_id=2323, last accessed 3 July 2013.

[12] Article 3 provides that when the personal data breach is likely to affect the personal data or privacy of a subscriber or individual, the provider shall, in addition to the notification referred to in Article 2, also notify the subscriber or individual of the breach.

[13] *EU: new regulation may harmonise telcos' breach notification timeframe* available at http://dataguidance.com/news.asp?id=2054, last accessed 3 July 2013.

Perhaps, the major question is whether users can now be more confident that the legal framework is sufficient to protect their data? In other words, the knowledge that any misuse of their personal data online or offline will incur major penalties on organisations that do not respect data protection laws?

Finally, it should be added that recital 63 and Article 3(2)(a) provides that non-EU data controllers that offers goods or services or monitor data subject's behaviour, there is a requirement to appoint a representative in the host country unless the third country has an adequate level of protection. There was a concern about activities by Instagram, photoservice which was bought by Facebook and employed 13 employees. The European Parliament took the view that it did not matter how many employees were employed but rather how many data subjects there were.[14]

On a separate topic, it has addressed cloud computing[15] where a small number of data controllers can be employed, who process large amounts of data and would be caught within these provisions (amended Recital 74).[16]

Although it is not clear whether the amendments are likely to be adopted at a European level, it is clear that UK and several other Member States are likely to oppose some of the changes through the Regulation and may result in the watering down of the Regulation.[17] For instance, the UK recently expressed its view to opt-out of the "right to be forgotten" and it is not certain whether the European Commission will accept this change.[18]

The Regulation has raised a vigorous debate amongst the Member States, the European Commission and policy makers on the balance to be drawn in protecting users' data online and data controllers' interests in processing users' data.

---

[14] Ibid., at p. 35.

[15] Ibid., at p. 40.

[16] Ibid.

[17] Clark, L. ICO warns against "prescriptive" EU data protection proposals available at http://www.wired.co.uk/news/archive/2013-03/26/ico-data-protection, dated 26 March 2013; Ashford, W. EU states likely to force changes to proposed data protection rules available at http://www.computerweekly.com/news/2240179233/EU-states-likely-to-force-changes-to-proposed-data-protection-rules, dated 7 March 2013.

[18] Bowcott, W. *Britain seeks opt-out of new European social media privacy laws* available at http://www.guardian.co.uk/technology/2013/apr/04/britain-opt-out-right-to-be-forgotten-law, dated 4 April 2013.

Chapter 7
Framework Decision 2005/222/JHA and the Directive Against Information Systems

Abstract This chapter will consider the Framework Decision 2005/222/JHA, its background and the forthcoming changes introduced by the Directive against Information Systems which will replace the Framework Decision. The latter was recently passed in 2013 following major amendments introduced by the European Parliament by 541 votes to 91 votes. The main changes under the Directive would be its breadth by covering attacks against Information Systems using botnets and DOS attacks and provide minimum rules for the definition of criminal offences and sanctions in the area of attacks against Information Systems.

Keywords Framework decision 2005/222/JHA • Directive against Information Systems

The framework decision 2005/222/JHA was passed to deal with attacks against Information Systems in 2005. The European Commission found that 20 Member States had made notable progress in transposing the decision into national law with seven still to take action. Its aim would be to harmonise criminal law across the EU to ensure that Europe's law enforcement and judicial authority can take action against this form of crime. Compliance of the Framework Decision was required by 16 March 2007.

The European Parliament has recently approved a Directive by 541 votes to 91 that would replace and update the Framework decision.[1] According to the European Economic and Social Committee,[2] the Directive shares the deep concern

---

[1] European Parliament. *Combating attacks against Information Systems* available at http://www.europarl.europa.eu/oeil/popups/ficheprocedure.do?id=587653, last accessed 16th March 2013.

[2] European Economic Social Committee, Opinion of the European Economic and Social Committee on the 'Proposal for a Directive of the European Parliament and of the Council on attacks against Information Systems and repealing Council Framework Decision 2005/222/JHA' COM(2010) 517 final—2010/0273 (COD) dated 23 July 2011.

of the Commission over the deep scale of cybercrime in Europe and the critical and potential damage being done to the economy. The opinion noted the disappointment that 17 of the 27 Member States have ratified the Cybercrime Convention (this is now 16 as UK has recently ratified the Cybercrime Convention).[3] It was also of the view that the Commission should proceed to draft a comprehensive EU legislation against cybercrime, a comprehensive framework which would be essential to the Digital Agenda and Europe 2020 and deal with the prevention, detection and education issues in addition to law enforcement and punishment. The opinion did acknowledge that there will be challenges on personal data security and privacy other than cybercrime. It was satisfied that the Directive would cover attacks against Information Systems using botnets and DOS attacks and would help to prosecute perpetrators that attempt to hide behind the anonymity in which sophisticated tools can provide.

The Directive on Attacks against the Information Systems[4] would include definitions of current offence. The main legal basis to be adopted would be Article 83(1) TFEU. The objective of the Directive would be to approximate the rules on criminal law in the Member State in the area of attacks against Information Systems within the EU and improve cooperation between the judicial and competent authorities including the police and other specialized law enforcement bodies of the Member States. Furthermore, the objective of the Directive[5] would be to provide minimum rules concerning the definition of criminal offences and the sanctions in the area of attacks against Information Systems.[6] The common definitions particularly of Information Systems and computer data was needed to adopt a consistent approach in the Member State to the application of the proposed Directive. A "without right" would be added under "definitions" which would mean that any access, interference, interception or any other conduct referred to in this Directive, not authorized by the owner or right holder would not be permitted under national legislation. Further clarity is provided by defining what "interception" is within the recitals of the Directive. It would cover both direct interception such as listening to devices to indirect interception to cover the use of electronic eavesdropping or tapping devices by technical means. It deals with offences such as illegal access to Information Systems, illegal system interference and illegal data inference as well as specific rules or the liability

[3] Ibid. See also UK Parliament. Attacks against Information Systems available at http://www.publications.parliament.uk/pa/cm201012/cmselect/cmeuleg/428-xxix/42815.htm, dated 8 June 2011.

4 Proposed Directive (COM) 2010/0273 517 final. See "Commission proposes boosting Europe's defences against cyberattacks" (2010) *EU Focus* 22.

[5] Report on the proposal for a Directive of the European Parliament and of the Council on attacks against Information Systems and repealing Council Framework 2005/222/JHA COM(2010)0517. http://www.europarl.europa.eu/sides/getDoc.do?type=REPORT&mode=XML&reference=A7-2013-224&language=EN, dated 19 June 2013.

[6] Ibid. See also *European Parliament debates on attacks against Information Systems* available at http://www.europarl.europa.eu/sides/getDoc.do?type=CRE&reference=20130703&secondRef=ITEM-018&language=EN&ring=A7-2013-0224, dated 3 July 2013.

of legal persons, jurisdiction and exchange of information. It would be punishable as a criminal offence for the intentional commission of the crime involving interference with the illegal system (Article 3). Similarly, aiding and abetting to commit an offence would be punishable as a criminal offence (Article 8). It has also laid down specific guidance on sanctions (Article 9). A maximum of at least 2 years for cases that are not minor (Article 9(2)). At least 3 years of imprisonment if the offence was committed intentionally (Article 9(3)) and a significant number of Information Systems were affected and a maximum penalty of at least 5 years of imprisonment for offences that were committed within the framework of a criminal organisation or causing serious damage or committed against a critical infrastructure information system (Article 9(4)). The Member State would decide what constitutes a minor case based on their law and practice. Where the offence committed was insignificant, then imposing a criminal penalty may not be necessary (Recital 11). If certain offences are committed by misusing personal data of another person in order to gain trust of a third party, it maybe regarded as circumstances aggravating.

Where the offence concerned related to identity theft, this type would require action at EU level in the form of horizontal EU instrument (recital 14). Whilst there is specific reference made to identity theft, it is questionable whether the Data Protection Regulation is sufficient to deal with the protection of identity? The only difference that may exist is that if there is a horizontal EU instrument, is whether this is likely to be made a criminal offence. Thus, strengthening further protection in this area.

The Directive makes specific reference to a national contact point which would ensure that Member States should have an operational national point of contact and make use of the existing network of operational points of contact 24 h a day, 7 days a week. Procedures should be in place to deal with urgent request within a maximum of 8 h.

Under the Treaty protocols, UK, Ireland and Denmark are exempted from enacting the Directive. UK has chosen, however to opt-in into the proposed Directive. This would mean that the UK laws on computer crime would have to be updated to conform to the EU Directive and interpretation of the legislative provisions under the Directive would therefore be subject to the Court of Justice jurisdiction (Article 267 Lisbon Treaty). According to Parker, 'cyberattacks pose a threat to the protection of personal data. It can be expected that the Directive will be welcomed by both law enforcement and data protection authorities it should serve hopefully to dissuade attacks as well as to ensure that cybercriminals, including those whose attacks target personal data, will face the threat of prosecution, imprisonment and financial penalties…Financial institutions are, and have long been, a prime target for cyberattacks (and they) can sometimes be frustrated by the failure of law enforcement to take effective steps to respond to attacks. The introduction of stronger penalties and requirements for improved cooperation will be welcomed by financial institutions'.[7]

---

[7] *EU: Proposed directive to harmonise penalties for cyber attacks* available at http://www. pitmans.com/news/eu-proposed-directive-to-harmonise-penalties-for-cyber-attacks, last accessed 30 July 2013.

The Directive is not without its critics. Clayton argued that there was enough laws to convict cyber criminals but not enough policemen.[8] It is the enforcement that was the main concern. Furthermore, some EU countries remained unconvinced for a need of an EU cyber security Directive and questioned why a voluntary approach was not considered and that the Directive would lead to inconsistencies for companies that operated in several EU member states.[9]

Similarly, cyberattacks that occur tend not to be traceable or difficult to trace back and the question of jurisdiction might be raised. In other words, how would it be possible to prosecute an anonymous criminal who commits an attack on computer systems or networks in a multiple number of countries in the EU? Recital 12c of the Directive provides some guidance on this by placing the onus on the Member State:

> (12c) In order to fight cybercrime effectively, it is necessary to increase the resilience of Information Systems by taking appropriate measures to protect them more effectively against Cyber attacks. Member States should take necessary measures to protect critical infrastructures from cyber attacks, as part of which they should consider the protection of their Information Systems and associated data. Ensuring an adequate level of protection and security of Information Systems by legal persons, for example in connection with the provision of publicly available electronic communications services in line with existing EU legislation on privacy andelectronic communication and data protection, forms an essential part of a comprehensive approach to effectively counteracting cybercrime. Appropriate levels of protection should be provided against reasonably identifiable threats and vulnerabilities in accordance with the state of the art for specific sectors and the specific data processing situations. The cost and burden of such protection should be proportionate to the likely damage a cyber attack would cause to those affected. Member States are encouraged to provide for relevant measures incurring liabilities in the context of their national law in cases where a legal person has clearly not provided an appropriate level of protection against cyber attacks.

According to recent developments, the Directive was approved by the European Parliament with some amendments. This is likely to be a significant development with specific legislation directed to cybersecurity.

The Directive is yet to be approved by the European Council. Once approved, it will be published in the Official Journal of the European Union and Member States will have 2 years to implement the Directive.[10]

---

[8] *Elusive cyber-attackers to face 5 years' jail* at http://www.euractiv.com/infosociety/elusive-cyber-attackers-face-years-jail-news-505521, date last accessed 4th May 2012.

[9] Member states reportedly unconvinced on need for EU Cybersecurity Directive available at http://www.bna.com/member-states-reportedly-n17179874317/, dated 3 June 2013.

[10] Hunton and Williams. European *Parliament adopts new legislation to fight cybercrime* available at http://www.huntonprivacyblog.com/2013/07/articles/european-parliament-adopts-new-legislation-to-fight-cyber-crime/, dated 5 July 2013.

Chapter 8
European Data Protection Supervisor's Opinion on Cybersecurity

Abstract The European Data Protection Supervisor (EDPS) has recently issued its opinion on the cybersecurity particularly his view of the Proposed Cybersecurity Directive. This chapter will cover the salient points of the EDPS's opinion in the context of cybersecurity.

Keywords European data protection supervisor • Cybersecurity • Data protection regulation

The European Data Protection Supervisor (EDPS) has recently issued its opinion on the cybersecurity particularly his view of the proposed Data Protection Regulation and the Proposed Cybersecurity Directive (which is discussed in Chap. 9). This chapter will cover the salient points of the EDPS's opinion in the context of cybersecurity.

This is in response to a joint communication to various bodies of the EU on a cybersecurity strategy. Although the EDPS has expressed its welcome to the comprehensive strategy and proposed Directive against Information Systems, he was also emphatic that in the pursuance of cybersecurity, it may also lead to an interference with individuals' rights to privacy and the protection of their personal data guaranteed within the ECHR and the TFEU and the Charter of Fundamental Rights (para. 11, p. 4). Proportionality was the key and that any interference with an individual's privacy should not be disproportionate. A balance needed to be drawn between the protection of individuals against cybersecurity threats and the protection of their privacy (p. 4).

The EDPS also referred to role played by data controllers with regard to data security measures as required under the current At. 17 of the Data Protection Directive. Similarly, Sect. 2.1 of the cyber security strategy also refers to the data protection framework to require data controllers to adhere to data protection requirements. Whilst this part is not contentious, the manner and the way in which data security breaches will have to be reported under the new Data Protection

Regulation will need to be consistent throughout the EU and where necessary further guidelines maybe necessary from the national Data Protection Authority of each Member State.

The EDPS was, however, of the view that the Cyber security strategy and Directive should better complement the Data Protection Directive and do not overlap with each other, a point that was discussed previously. Furthermore, the EDPS was critical of the notable absence or mention of Data Protection Authorities in the implementation and enforcement of obligations laid down under the Cybersecurity strategy (p. 5).

The proposed Data Protection Regulation was not mentioned within the Cybersecurity strategy nor the proposals for a Regulation on electronic identification and trust services for electronic transactions in the internal market. The EDPS was of the view that as a result of the failure to recognise the significance of the Data Protection Regulation and the Regulation on electronic identification, the cybersecurity strategy does not provide a 'comprehensive and holistic view of cybersecurity in the EU and risks to perpetuate a fragmented and compartmentalized approach' (p. 5).

The EDPS did note that there were express references to privacy and data protection within the strategy (p. 6) such as The sharing of data should be compliant with EU law. The EDPS noted, however, a lack of specific mention of privacy and data protection requirements in the fight against cyber criminality and cyber defence policy.

The EDPS was also of the view that Data Protection Authorities had a role to play in all aspects of the Cybersecurity Strategy and not merely awareness to raising actions and to the proposed Directive on NIS (p. 6).

Although acknowledging that the aim of the cyber security strategy to establish a holistic approach to 'cyber resilience, cybercrime and cyberdefence', the EDPS took the view that from a data protection perspective, cyber resilience and the fight against cybercrime can protect personal data in cyberspace (p. 7). However, the EDPS was critical that the definitions of 'cyber security', 'cyber resilience', 'cyber crime' and 'cyberdefence' needed to be clearly defined in the Joint Communication to avoid any ambiguity and ensure that there was a common level of understanding. This is particularly relevant where an individual's privacy was likely to be compromised (p. 7).

The EDPS was also critical of the absence of any reference to data protection law in the fight against cybercrime and cyber defence policy. Examples where cybercrime is likely to be relevant include the collecting, exchanging and using personal data of individual's IP addresses and those victims of crime and suspected offenders. The EDPS was of the view that any collection of personal data for the purposes of investigation and prosecution of crimes should comply with the data protection requirements laid down under the Council Decision 2008/977/JHA. This is likely to be replaced by a forthcoming Directive on the processing of personal data in the area of police and judicial cooperation in criminal matters (p. 9).

Furthermore, the EDPS was emphatic about the need to define appropriate data protection safeguards and that any sharing of information between the relevant stakeholders of the strategy on cybercrime, cyberdefence and EU external relations had to be clarified.

As alluded to earlier, the absence of the role of Data Protection Authorities as relevant players within cybersecurity was criticised by the EDPS. To recap, Data Protection Authorities oversee the compliance of data protection laws within their Member States. The Strategy names NIS Authorities/CERTs, law enforcement and defence authorities and ENISA. According to the EDPS, the Data Protection Authorities, in their capacity as supervisory bodies should also supervise pilot project on fighting botnets and Malware. The EDPS also encouraged the exchange of beset practice in awareness in the field of cybersecurity.

As the EDPS also considered the Cybersecurity Directive, his views are analysed in more detail in Chap. 10.

Chapter 9
Cybersecurity Directive 2013

Abstract This chapter will consider the Cybersecurity Directive introduced by the European Commission with the aim of dealing with cybersecurity breaches and disruptions to cyber networks. In a recent 2012 survey, the Eurobrometer on Cybersecurity found that 38 % of EU Internet users were concerned with the safety of online payments. The Directive also aims to create Computer Emergency Response Teams (known as "CERTS") on handling the number of data security breaches. It will consider what its role will be as provided by the Directive and consider shortcomings of CERT as recently highlighted by ENISA.

Keywords Cybersecurity directive • Cyberattacks • ENISA • CERTs

In a separate and significant development, the European Commissioner introduced a Cybersecurity Directive. According to the European Commissioner, Neelie Kroes, "we are creating incentives for private companies to improve their track records in network security, and helping national governments to use the learning from this to improve overall national capabilities" [1].

Contu, a research Director for Gartner took the view that "if you compare the regulatory landscape in Europe with the US, it's not as regulated here [1]".

To give some background, according to [2] it was reported that amongst organisations that were recently cyberattacked it included Apple, Facebook and Twitter [2]. Breaches of Citibank and Nasdaq and Mastercard indicated vulnerability to cyberattacks [2]. In 2011, statistics by Symnantic had shown an 81 % increase in malicious attacks [2]. It is against this background that legislation is being introduced. Futhermore, the European Commission was not convinced that the current voluntary approach provides sufficient protection against network and information security incidents and risks across the EU and was insufficient to keep pace with the fast changing landscape of threats. According to Neelie Kroes, "Europe needs resilient systems and networks. Failing to act would impose significant costs: on consumers, on business, on society" [3].

R. Wong, *Data Security Breaches and Privacy in Europe*, SpringerBriefs in Cybersecurity, 39
DOI: 10.1007/978-1-4471-5586-7_9, © The Author(s) 2013

The Directive would require the disclosure and sharing of information between authorities set up in the Member State supported by ENISA and the new Europol Cybercrime Centre known as the "Network and Information Security" (NIS) Directive, the aim would be for the EU to prevent and respond to cyber disruptions and attacks. In a recent survey dated 2012, the Eurobarometer on Cybersecurity found that 38 % of EU Internet users were concerned with the safety of online payments [4].

The Directive would:

1. Set minimum levels of national capabilities by establishing competent authority for network and information security (NIS).
2. Set up Computer Emergency Response Teams (CERTs)
3. Adopt national NIS strategies and national NIS cooperation plans.

Based on Article 114 TFEU, the EU can adopt measures for the approximation of the provisions laid down by law regulation or administrative action in Member States.

The Cybersecurity Directive would complement other Directives. Namely, the Directive 2002/21/EC (Framework Directive) on the definition of publicly available electronic communication. It would have parallel similarities with the DPEC and the proposed Data Protection Regulation to deal with security of personal data. Recital 31 of the Cybersecurity Directive lays emphasis on the compromisation of personal data. Co-operation between authorities (set up under the Cybersecurity Directive) and Data Protection Authorities to address personal data breaches.

There was an obligation on Member State(s) to prevent, handle and respond to risks and incidents affecting networks and information systems (Article 1(2)(a)).

The Directive would not apply where it overlaps with the DPEC (Article 1(3)) and is without prejudice to the Data Protection Directive 95/46/EC and DPEC and DPEC (Article 1(5)).

The Member State can impose higher levels of protection than the minimum provided under the Cybersecurity Directive (Article 2).

The definitions provided under Article 3 on security is defined to cover "the ability of a network and information system to resist at a given level of confidence, accident or malicious action that compromise the availability, authenticity, integrity and confidentiality of stored or transmitted data or the related services offered by or accessible via that network and information system" (Article 3(2)).

A national network and information security strategy would be covered under Article 5.

The responsibilities of the authorities set up to oversee network and information security would be defined under Article 6. Each Member State would be required to set up a body to deal with security of network and information systems.

The authorities would be expected to co-operate with the Data Protection Authorities.

A CERT would be set up to deal with the handling of incidents and risk (Article 7).

The Commission and the authorities would be expected to form a network to co-operate against risks and incidents affecting network and information systems (Article 8). This would be further supported by guidance provided by ENISA.

ENISA recently issued a report highlighting 16 shortcomings with CERT including detection of incidents, data quality, slow delivery and lack of contextual information and that a major problem to CERT's activities would be to comply with data privacy regulations.[1] ENISA recommended a more proactive approach to data security and a number of technologies need to be used more such as deploying their sensor networks or honeypot technologies.[2]

The Directive could cover "market operators". These are defined as e-commerce platforms, Internet payment gateways, social networks, search engine, cloud computers and application providers.

At present, there are doubts whether the Cybersecurity Directive would pass before the European Parliament [5]. The key issue appears to be whether those operators affected would be expected to make official notification indicating that they have been cyberattacked under the new rules. Computers have to ensure they have IT suitable security mechanisms in place.

As any organisation that provides any services online would have to ensure information security, the Directive could include other online providers such as Skype. They would be expected to report breaches of personal data, but also there would be a separate obligation to report all other data breaches in the interests of Cybersecurity.

---

[1] *Security reports says EU needs more 'honeypots' to lure cyberattackers* available at http://www.euractiv.com/specialreport-cybersecurity/europe-needs-honeypots-trap-cybe-news-518279?utm_source=EurActiv%20Newsletter&utm_campaign=173af7e866-newsletter_daily_update&utm_medium=email, dated 5 March 2013 and ENISA *Proactive detection of security incidents* available at http://www.enisa.europa.eu/activities/cert/support/proactive-detection, last accessed 30 July 2013.

[2] ENISA *op. cit.* n. 109.

References

1. Fonatanella-Khan J, McCarthy B (2013) Companies face cyber security law. http://www. ft.com/cms/s/0/53914414-6187-11e2-9545-00144feab49a.html#axzz2QeogNea8. Accessed 18 Jan 2013
2. Hiller JS, Russell RS (2013) The challenge and imperative of private sector cybersecurity: an international comparison. Comput Law Secur Rev 29(3):236–245
3. Fontanella-Khan J (2013) Cyber security legislation: data safety and privacy must be balanced. http://www.ft.com/cms/s/0/0f9189e8-c93a-11e2-9d2a-00144feab7de.html#axzz2Vv32bDA5. Accessed 6 June 2013
4. Cybersecurity Directive (2013) http://ec.europa.eu/information_society/newsroom/cf/dae/ document.cfm?doc_id=1666, p 3
5. Cybersecurity Directive faces uncertain fate in Parliament (2013) http://www.euractiv.com/s pecialreport-cybersecurity/cybersecurity-directive-faces-pa-news-518314. Accessed 7 March 2013

Chapter 10
Criticism of the Cybersecurity Directive

Abstract This chapter argues that the Cybersecurity Directive will be unworkable in practice and considers the reasons and shortcomings of this Directive. In particular, the definition of "market operators" is very broad to include search engines and social media. Sanctions for non-compliance will apply. A further criticism is that there is no obligation to notify citizens of data security breaches within the Directive, but rather the obligation is placed on market operators to notify and make data breaches public. There is a further scepticism over how the Cybersecurity Directive will be put into practice.

Keywords Cybersecurity directive • EDRI • Data breach notifications

The main criticisms leveled at the Cybersecurity Directive by businesses and academics are that it is costly, unworkable in practice and exceeds the powers provided under the Data Retention Directive [1].

According to Hiller and Russell, the Cybersecurity Directive is a distributed problem. It establishes standards for security, encouraging voluntary coordination between public and private entities, educational efforts and threat information sharing and protection of citizen's privacy.[1]

The definition of "market operators" is very broad to include search engines, social media and cloud providers. Sanctions for non-compliance will apply. According to the EDRI, [2] there is an attempt to "miliarise security" in cyberspace. This was seen in some member states such as the UK which had allocated £640 million to cyber security from 2011 to 2015. The Directive was described by EDRI as being unworkable in practice conferring powers on a single national competent authority. The Directive would encourage one single agency to acquire primary in each Member State and undermine constitutional arrangements that various states have for the separation of powers and accountability. [2] There was a concern that it would grant draconian powers to ENISA

---

[1] Hiller and Russell, op. cit. n. 96.

R. Wong, *Data Security Breaches and Privacy in Europe*, SpringerBriefs in Cybersecurity,   43
DOI: 10.1007/978-1-4471-5586-7_10, © The Author(s) 2013

and Member States exceeding those granted under the Data Retention Directive and challenged successfully before the Constitutional Courts. [2] There was a further question whether the Directive would be compatible with Article 8 of the European Convention of Human Rights? The Directive was likely to be burdensome to comply by the industry. According to Nauwelaerts, "the possible impact of the proposed rules on security requirements and incident reporting should not be underestimated, as under the proposed regime public bodies, as well as private actors, would need to ensure security of the networks and systems over which they have 'control'", said Mr Nauwelaerts. "How this will translate practically in today's cloud computing environments, for example, remains to be seen" [3].

A further criticism of the Directive is that there is no obligation to notify citizens of data security breaches. For instance, Article 14 of the Directive place an obligation on market operators to notify, but no obligation to make data breaches public.

> 1. Member States shall ensure that public administrations and market operators take appropriate technical and organisational measures to manage the risks posed to the security of the networks and information systems which they control and use in their operations. Having regard to the state of the art, these measures shall guarantee a level of security appropriate to the risk presented. In particular, measures shall be taken to prevent and minimise the impact of incidents affecting their network and information system on the core services they provide and thus ensure the continuity of the services underpinned by those networks and information systems.
>
> 2. Member States shall ensure that *public administrations and market operators notify to the competent authority* incidents having a significant impact on the security of the core services they provide.
>
> 3. The requirements under para. 1 and 2 apply to all market operators providing services within the European Union.

Competent authorities may notify if they determine it is in the public interest (Article 14(4)). The question is what constitutes "public interest" over when to disclose or not? Furthermore, powers are conferred under Article 15 to market operators and public administrations as follows:

> 1. Member States shall ensure that the competent authorities have the power to require market operators and public administrations to:
>
>   (a) provide information needed to assess the security of their networks and information systems, including documented security policies;
>
>   (b) undergo a security audit carried out by a qualified independent body or national authority and make the results thereof available to the competent authority.
>
> 2. Member States shall ensure that competent authorities have the power to issue binding instructions to market operators and public administrations.
>
> 3. The competent authorities shall notify incidents of a suspected serious criminal nature to law enforcement authorities.
>
> 4. The competent authorities shall work in close cooperation with personal data protection authorities when addressing incidents resulting in personal data breaches.
>
> 5. Member States shall ensure that any obligations imposed on public administrations and market operators under this Chapter may be subject to judicial review.

Further criticisms of the Cybersecurity Directive is the vagueness in reporting cyberattacks which does very little to protect the EU citizen's data held outside the EU [4].

According to Nauwelaerts, the Directive is likely to raise a number of legal issues and added his scepticism in how this can be put into practice [4].

> We are going to have to export European rules in that respect... If they are only from Europe I'm not sure they are going to solve global problems [4].

Anderson takes the view that the Directive is another step towards the millitarisation of cyberspace citing that most of the critical infrastructure of cybersecurity are in the hands of foreign companies and 'that moving cyberscurity cooperation from the current loose association of private–public partnerships to a centralized classified system will make it harder for most of them to play' [5].

On the other hand, Digital Europe welcomed the Directive to strength public sector agencies and improve pan-European co-ordination, but took the view that it would be a move away from the voluntary biodirectional information sharing between mandatory obligations and unidirectional reporting requirements.[2] More safeguards were needed to be put in place and measures to be adopted should be proportionate in terms of sectors targeted.[3]

In a recent opinion published by the EDPS, he welcomed the fact that there was express reference made to the data protection framework under Article 1(5) of the Cybersecurity Directive [6]. However, the EDPS was critical that the interaction between the current and future data protection legal frameworks with the Cybersecurity Directive was not analysed in more detail and it was not clear how this interaction would work. The EDPS raised several questions on the relationship between the security obligations within the Cybersecurity Directive and that they should ensure to be within the current and future data protection frameworks. Other questions include the obligations of NIS competent authorities on the level of confidentiality and security that they should ensure they receive under the new incident notification procedure [7]. The EDPS further emphasized the need to embed data protection by design by default (see chap 4). The EDPS has advised that a provision should be included within the Cybersecurity Directive to consider data protection from the early stage of the design through the lifecycle of processes, procedures, organisations, techniques and infrastructures involved [7].

The EDPS further noted the overlap of data security obligations under the Cybersecurity Directive and under the EU legal framework for providers of electronic communications networks and services [6]. The EDPS has advised that integrated approach to security would be necessary to mitigate risks for network information systems. According to the EDPS, this was particularly important within an interconnected digital environment.

In the context of "market operators", the EDPS was of the view that this was not clearly defined in an exhaustive manner [6]. The Cybersecurity Directive could be extended to other players in a non-harmonised manner by Member States. It was questioned why certain sectors were given a significant role in network and information security, but not others such as manufacturers of hardware and software or

---

[2] Digital Europe., op. cit. n. 93.

[3] See footnote 2.

providers of security software and services. It was not clear whether EU institutions such as European Parliament would be covered by this Directive and this needed to be clearer. More clarity was needed on Article 3(8) on the definition of market operators and there should be an exhaustive list of relevant stakeholders [8]. A further point was the confusion that would be generated between this Directive and the Directive 2002/21/EC where certain operators are excluded from the Cybersecurity Directive, but not Directive 2002/21/EC. Further clarity was needed.

The EDPS was also of the view that "network and information system" needed more clarity. Did this phrase cover private local networks that were not connected to the Internet? Connected with this, are intranets (deliberate blocking of internet access within firewalls) also excluded from the Directive? If the Commission did intend to exclude private networks, the EDPS recommended that this should be made clearer in Article 3(1). Furthermore, "incident" (within Article 3(4)) in relation to security should be clarified. Would an unsuccessful attack be considered an "incident"? The EDPS pointed out that in the context of data security breach, Article 4(9) of the Regulation required this to lead to a consequence such as loss of data (p. 15).

The EDPS also pointed out that the obligation to establish a risk assessment plan under Article 5(2) was too narrow as this did not over prioritization and treatment including the criteria for possible countermeasures. The EDPS recommended that a risk management framework should be created which would include a risk assessment phase [9].

The EDPS further pointed out the need to involve data protection authorities within the definition and implementation of NIS strategies [6]. CERTs should also be involved in the compliance of data protection rules and CERTs may seek cooperation from data protection authorities in the context of protecting personal data.

The EDPS was emphatic about the need for the Directive to provide sufficient clarity on notification requirements and the content and form is not defined clearly within the Directive. The EDPS further recommended that sufficient safeguards should be in place to ensure that adequate protection of the data processed by NIS competent authorities [10].

According to the EDPS, incident notifications should be applied without prejudice to personal data breach notification obligations pursuant to relevant data protection laws [11].

It further added that any disclosure of information to the public of information concerning the incident should not contain any personal information and that public interest would be effectively pursued by disclosing only anonymous or effectively anonymised information under Article 14 [10]. Any disclosure of personal information will require a balance between the different interests of stakeholders [6].

In connection with this, personal data maybe exchanged with NIS competent authorities such as names and IP addresses [12]. Although IP addresses do not identify the individual, it is possible through indirect means and therefore could still constitute the processing of "personal data". Therefore, data protection rules would still apply. Article 7 of the Data Protection Directive which provides the appropriate legal basis should be followed [6].

The EDPS has made several recommendations to the Directive, the key points have been discussed above. Given the number of recommendations, the Directive is still at its embryonic stage and much work is still required before this is fully revised.

At present, negotiations for the Directive between the Council and the Commission are complex and it is anticipated that the Directive would be delayed [6].

In terms of the response to the Directive (other than the EDPS), there is a mixed response. On the one hand, it appears that the Directive was introduced with the aim to address a lacuna in the regulatory framework on cybersecurity and introduce responsibilities on cybersecurity incidents. On the other hand, there are questions raised whether this should be introduced at a European level (principle of "subsidiarity") rather than leave it to the Member States to deal with the issue. It is further complicated by the coverage to include non-EU organisations to deal with cybersecurity incidents and there is considerable overlap with the DPEC and the proposed Data Protection Regulation and may go further than the Data Protection framework. The rules would be too broad and would not have the effect of boosting cybersecurity in Europe. According to Wagner, Security and Privacy Policy Manager of TechAmerica's Europe arm,

> We believe that to be manageable, useful and proportionate, the requirements should be narrowly targeted at sectors which operate truly critical infrastructures [13].

It is likely to have an impact on non-EU service providers particularly for Internet companies [14]. For instance, online travel services would be required to report an attack that prevents users from booking travel arrangements [14]. It will depend on how the Directive would be implemented by the Member States.

One of the problems highlighted recently was the reluctance on the part of organisations to report data security breaches of its of effects on its reputation and share price and the difficulty for organisations to share information about cyberattacks with government or organisations [15]. There is a risk that even with legislation, organisations may look the other way and pretend that an attack had not occurred [15]. The UK government for instance has set up voluntary collaboration between private and public sectors, but whether it will work will depend on factors such as confidence that organisations have to prevent the information they give being leaked. However, it is questionable whether the Directive would increase transparency on cybersecurity arrangements and whether the number of cyberattacks will lead to a reporting fatigue to the relevant authorities.

References

1. EDRI (2013) *Questions on the Draft Directive on Cybersecurity Strategy* available at http://www.edri.org/edrigram/number11.1/cybersecurity-draft-directive-eu. Accessed 16th Jan 2013
2. Digital Rights in Europe (2013) *Questions on the draft directive on Cybersecurity Strategy* available at http://www.edri.org/edrigram/number11.1/cybersecurity-draft-directive-eu, Accessed 16 Jan 2013
3. Fontanella-Khan, J(2013) *Cyber security legislation: data safety and privacy must be balanced* available at http://www.ft.com/cms/s/0/0f9189e8-c93a-11e2-9d2a-00144feab7de.html#axzz2Vv32bDA5, Accessed 6 Jun 2013

4. *Storm cloud emerges from EU cybersecurity strategy (2013)* available at http://www.euractiv. com/infosociety/stormcloud-emerges-cloud-safety-news-517658?utm_source=EurActiv%20 Newsletter&utm_campaign=40fee23980-newsletter_infosociety&utm_medium=email, last Accessed 8 Feb 2013

5. *EU cybersecurity directive considered harmful (2013)* available at http://www.lightbluetouchpape r.org/2013/02/08/eu-cyber-security-directive-considered-harmful/, last Accessed 30 July 2013

6. European Data Protection Supervisor (2013) Opinion of the European Data Protection Supervisor on Cybersecurity Strategy available at https://secure.edps.europa.eu/EDPSWEB/webdav/shared/ Documents/Consultation/Opinions/2013/13-06-14_Cyber_security_EN.pdf, last Accessed 14 Aug 2013

7. European Data Protection Supervisor (2013) Opinion of the European Data Protection Supervisor on Cybersecurity Strategy available at https://secure.edps.europa.eu/EDPSWEB/webdav/shared/ Documents/Consultation/Opinions/2013/13-06-14_Cyber_security_EN.pdf, last Accessed 14 Aug 2013, p. 13

8. European Data Protection Supervisor (2013) Opinion of the European Data Protection Supervisor on Cybersecurity Strategy available at https://secure.edps.europa.eu/EDPSWEB/webdav/shared/ Documents/Consultation/Opinions/2013/13-06-14_Cyber_security_EN.pdf, last Accessed 14 Aug 2013, p. 14

9. European Data Protection Supervisor (2013) Opinion of the European Data Protection Supervisor on Cybersecurity Strategy available at https://secure.edps.europa.eu/EDPSWEB/webdav/shared/ Documents/Consultation/Opinions/2013/13-06-14_Cyber_security_EN.pdf, last Accessed 14 Aug 2013, p. 15

10. European Data Protection Supervisor (2013) Opinion of the European Data Protection Supervisor on Cybersecurity Strategy available at https://secure.edps.europa.eu/EDPSWEB/webdav/shared/ Documents/Consultation/Opinions/2013/13-06-14_Cyber_security_EN.pdf, last Accessed 14 Aug 2013, p. 17

11. European Data Protection Supervisor (2013) Opinion of the European Data Protection Supervisor on Cybersecurity Strategy available at https://secure.edps.europa.eu/EDPSWEB/webdav/shared/ Documents/Consultation/Opinions/2013/13-06-14_Cyber_security_EN.pdf, last Accessed 14 Aug 2013, p. 16

12. European Data Protection Supervisor (2013) Opinion of the European Data Protection Supervisor on Cybersecurity Strategy available at https://secure.edps.europa.eu/EDPSWEB/webdav/shared/ Documents/Consultation/Opinions/2013/13-06-14_Cyber_security_EN.pdf, last Accessed 14 Aug 2013, p. 18

13. Martinez, J (2013) *Tech associations raise concerns with EU's proposed cybersecurity rules* available at http://thehill.com/blogs/hillicon-valley/technology/281783-tech-associations-raise-concerns-with-eus-proposed-cybersecurity-rules. Accessed 7 Feb 2013

14. King, R (2013) *New EU Cybersecurity Directive to impact US companies* available at http://blogs.wsj.com/cio/2013/02/07/new-eu-cyber-security-directive-to-impact-u-s-compa-nies/. Accessed 7 Feb 2013

15. Blitz, J (2013) Francis Maude interview: UK takes voluntary approach to sharing informa-tion on cyber attacks available at http://www.ft.com/cms/s/0/594bdac2-c938-11e2-9d2a-00144feab7de.html#axzz2Vv32bDA5. Accessed 6 Jun 2013

Chapter 11
Concluding Remarks

Abstract This chapter will conclude by revisiting the original aims of this book. Namely, to consider the goals of data protection and explore the application and relevance in the cybersecurity context. Although data protection is primarily concerned with the protection of an individual's personal data, a cyber attack or a data security breach can inevitably lead to the loss of data involving an individual's personal information. Whilst cybersecurity continues to be a high priority on the government's agenda, it is perfectly conceivable whether the existing framework (through the Cybercrime Convention and the European EU Electronic Communications framework and the Cybersecurity Directive and Data Protection Regulation) can at least address some of the shortcomings. It will conclude that any proposed change in the Regulator's role to enforce the laws will be a challenging one.

Keywords Cybersecurity • Cyberattack • Data protection • ENISA • Personal data

The aim of this chapter was to revisit the goals of data protection and explore the application and relevance in the cybersecurity context. Although data protection is primarily concerned with the protection of an individual's personal data (be it their identity or a broader view of their legal right to "personality"), a cyber attack or a data security breach can inevitably lead to the loss of data involving an individual's personal information. This is more so, when viewed in the context of a criminal activity such as hacking perpetrated by an individual within a cybercrime context or to the other end of the spectrum, another breach of another country's database.

It was shown that there is likely to be a considerable overlap between the Cybersecurity Directive and the Data Protection Regulation and the emphasis on the notification of security breaches. Not least, there has been criticism over the breadth of the Cybersecurity Directive to cover "market providers" (Internet providers). Its coverage is likely to extend to non-EU providers and the rationale is

R. Wong, *Data Security Breaches and Privacy in Europe*, SpringerBriefs in Cybersecurity,   49
DOI: 10.1007/978-1-4471-5586-7_11, © The Author(s) 2013

questioned for not leaving this area self-regulated through voluntary arrangements in light of recent cyber attacks. Although the Cybersecurity Directive has laid down obligations on data breach notifications for Internet and telecommunication service providers, there is no obligation to notify EU citizens unless it is in the public interest. Furthermore, there is likely to be an overlap with the proposed Data Protection Regulation (on data breach notifications), which is likely to lead to more confusion amongst organisations and therefore, clarity will be imperative. This final point was further reinforced by the EDPS's recent opinion.

It should not be forgotten that there has been considerable work conducted by ENISA, which was set up to examine, amongst other issues, cybersecurity. Regulation 580/2011[1] was passed to amend Regulation 460/2004 that created ENISA. It has produced position papers and guidelines dealing with botnets and the like. Furthermore, it has recently identified shortcomings with CERT and its need to take a more proactive approach to its use of honeypot traps.

Although cybersecurity continues to be a high priority on the government's agenda, it is perfectly conceivable whether the existing framework (through the Cybercrime Convention and the European EU Electronic Communications framework and the Cyber security Directive and Data Protection Regulation) can at least address some of the shortcomings. Whether this could be extended to non-EEA countries would depend on the effectiveness of the laws that implement the Cybersecurity Directive.

Any proposed change in the Regulator's role to enforce the laws and how this can be applied more effectively particularly against non-EU providers is likely to be a challenging one. Indeed, it is arguable that the regulatory field on cybersecurity and data protection has reached saturated point that there is enough regulation to deal with the issues, but what is required is more awareness and education to comprehend the scale and magnitude of cyber attacks and for regulators to use the powers to enforce the regulation.

---

[1] Regulation 580/2011 of the European Parliament and of the Council of 8 June 2011 amending Regulation (EC) No 460/2004 establishing the European Network and Information Security Agency as regards its duration, OJ L165/3, dated 24 June 2011. "At the time of writing, a draft opinion had been published by the European Parliament Civil Liberties, Justice and Home Affairs (LIBE) Committee to deal with the general notification of data security breaches. It was emphasized that the EU cybersecurity legislation should follow the adoption of the General Data Protection Regulation, not precede it." For more information, see Out-Law news: Data protection reform should precede Network and Information Security Directive, says MEP available at http://www.out-law.com/en/articles/2013/september/data-protection-reforms-should-precede-network-and-information-security-directive-says-mep/, dated 5 September 2013.

Bibliographies

1. AlertBoot (2011) UK private sector breaches up 58% YOY. http://www.ico.gov.uk/about_us/research/~/media/documents/library/Corporate/Research_and_reports/annual_track_2011_organisations.ashx. Accessed 9 Nov 2011
2. Art.29 Working Party (2011) The future of privacy, WP 168. http://ec.europa.eu/justice/policies/privacy/docs/wpdocs/2009/wp168_en.pdf. Accessed 1 Dec 2011
3. Ashford W (2013) How will cyber security directive affect business. http://www.computerweekly.com/news/2240178256/How-will-EU-cybersecurity-directive-affect-business. Accessed 19 Feb 2013
4. Baker LB, Finkle J (2011) Sony PlayStation suffers massive data breach. http://www.reuters.com/article/2011/04/26/us-sony-stoldendata-idUSTRE73P6WB20110426. Accessed 26 April 2011
5. BBC news (2008) Timeline: child benefits records loss. http://news.bbc.co.uk/1/hi/7104368.stm. Dated 25 June 2008
6. Cagnazzo L, Taticchi P, Fuiano F (2011) Impacts of ISO 9000 on business performances: a literature review. http://unipg.academia.edu/LucaCagnazzo/Papers/193302/Impacts_of_ISO_9000_on_Business_Performances_a_Literature_Review. Accessed 21 Oct 2011
7. Chandler JA (2007) Negligence liability for breaches of data security. http://papers.ssrn.com/sol3/papers.cfm?abstract_id=1268926. Accessed July 2007
8. Citizens Directive 2009/136/EC. http://eur-lex.europa.eu/LexUriServ/LexUriServ.do?uri=OJ:L:2009:337:0011:0036:En:PDF. Accessed Dec 2011
9. Commission proposes boosting Europe's defences against cyberattacks (2010) EU Focus 22
10. Convention on Cybercrime. http://conventions.coe.int/Treaty/Commun/ChercheSig.asp?NT=185&CM=8&DF=&CL=ENG. Accessed 3 Jan 2013
11. Data Protection Regulation. http://ec.europa.eu/justice/data-protection/document/review2012/com_2012_11_en.pdf. Accessed 25 Jan 2012
12. EastWest Institute (2011) The Second Worldwide Cybersecurity Summit. http://www.ewi.info/second-worldwide-cybersecurity-summit. Accessed Dec 2011
13. EastWest Institute (2011) Protecting the digital economy: the first worldwide Cybersecurity Summit in Dallas, 2011. http://www.ewi.info/dallas
14. Elusive cyber-attackers to face 5 years' jail. http://www.euractiv.com/infosociety/elusive-cyber-attackers-face-years-jail-news-505521. Accessed 4 May 2012
15. EDRI, ENDitorial (2013) Questions on the draft directive on cyber security strategy. http://www.edri.org/edrigram/number11.1/cybersecurity-draft-directive-eu. Accessed 16 Jan 2013
16. ENISA: General FAQ on ENISA. http://www.enisa.europa.eu/media/faq-on-enisa/general-faqs-on-enisa. Accessed 4 Jan 2013

17. ENISA, Position paper on Botnets. http://www.enisa.europa.eu/doc/pdf/deliverables/enisa_pp_botnets.pdf. Accessed 4 Jan 2013
18. ENISA (2013) Protecting Europe's citizens against cyber attacks. http://www.enisa.europa.eu/media/key-documents/fact-sheets/Cyber_Attacks_2008_May-1.pdf. Accessed 4 Jan 2013
19. ENISA, Security measures and breaches. http://www.enisa.europa.eu/doc/pdf/deliverables/enisa_pp_strengthening_eu_legislation.pdf. Accessed 4 Jan 2013
20. ENISA, Resilience of Europe's e-communications. http://www.enisa.europa.eu/pages/resilience.htm. Accessed 4 Jan 2013
21. ENISA, Study on security and anti-spam measures. http://www.enisa.europa.eu/pages/spam/doc/enisa_spam_study_2007.pdf. Accessed 4 Jan 2013
22. Europa, Privacy Enhancing Technologies (PETs). http://europa.eu/rapid/press-release_MEMO-07-159_en.htm. Accessed 2 May 2007
23. European Commission: Review of the data protection legal framework. http://ec.europa.eu/justice/policies/privacy/review/index_en.htm. Accessed 21 Oct 2011
24. European Commission (2011) Commission's first report on the transposition of the Data Protection Directive. http://ec.europa.eu/justice/policies/privacy/lawreport/report_en.htm. Accessed Dec 2011
25. European Commission (2010) Communication from the Commission to the European Parliament, the Council, the Economic and Social Committee and the Committee of the Regions: A comprehensive approach on personal data in the European Union, COM(2010) 609 final, 7
26. European Commission (2012) European Commission proposes a comprehensive reform of the data protection rules. http://ec.europa.eu/justice/newsroom/data-protection/news/120125_en.htm. Accessed 25 Jan 2012
27. European Commission (2013) Proposal for a European Regulation. http://statewatch.org/news/2011/dec/eu-com-draft-dp-reg-inter-service-consultation.pdf. Accessed 4 Jan 2013
28. European Economic Social Committee (2011) Opinion of the European Economic and Social Committee on the 'Proposal for a Directive of the European Parliament and of the Council on attacks against information systems and repealing Council Framework Decision 2005/222/JHA' COM(2010) 517 final—2010/0273 (COD), 23 July 2011
29. Expert warns on cyberwar threat. http://www.upi.com/Science_News/2012/03/16/Expert-warns-on-cyberwar-threat/UPI-33781331937216/. Accessed 16 March 2012
30. Feisted A (2011) Data security: breaches can result in huge costs. Financial Times. http://www.ft.com/cms/s/0/beac7484-04c8-11e1-b309-00144feabdc0.html#axzz1gn1UfhFn. Accessed 8 Nov 2011
31. Fontanella-Khan J, McCarthy B (2013) Companies face EU cyber security law. http://www.ft.com/cms/s/0/53914414-6187-11e2-9545-00144feab49a.html#axzz2QeogNea8. Accessed 18 Jan 2013
32. Goldsmith J (2013) Cybersecuity Treaties: a sceptical view. http://media.hoover.org/sites/default/files/documents/FutureChallenges_Goldsmith.pdf. Accessed 4 Jan 2013
33. Guardian Technology Blog (2011) Sony suffers second data breach with theft of 25m more user details. http://www.guardian.co.uk/technology/blog/2011/may/03/sony-data-breach-online-entertainment. Accessed 19 Dec 2011
34. ICO (2010) Report data breaches or risk tougher sanctions, warns the ICO. www.ico.gov.uk/~/media/documents/.../data_breaches_260110.ashx. Accessed 27 Jan 2010
35. ICO on Data security breach management. www.ico.gov.uk/.../data_protection/.../guidance_on_data_security_br.... Accessed July 2011
36. ICO (2010) 1000 data breaches reported to the ICO. http://www.ico.gov.uk/~/media/documents/pressreleases/2010/1000_DATA_BREACHES280510.ashx. Accessed 28 May 2010 and ICO
37. ICO: Likely breaches of the DPA received between 6 April 2010 and 22 March 2011, by sector. http://www.ico.gov.uk/about_us/how_we_comply/disclosure_log/~/media/documents/disclosure_log/IRQ0382403b.ashx. Accessed 15 April 2011

38. ICO Report on the Annual findings of the Information Commissioner's Office, Annual Track, 2011. http://www.ico.gov.uk/about_us/research/~/media/documents/library/Corporate/Research_and_reports/annual_track_2011_organisations.ashx. Accessed 9 Feb 2012

39. King R (2013) New EU cyber security directive to impact US companies http://blogs.wsj.com/cio/2013/02/07/new-eu-cyber-security-directive-to-impact-u-s-companies/. Accessed 7 Feb 2013

40. Lemos R (2001) International Cybercrime Treaty finalized. http://news.cnet.com/2100-1001-268894.html. Accessed 22 June 2001

41. Leonhard W (2011) What the latest data security breaches really mean. http://www.infoworld.com/t/data-security/what-the-latest-data-security-breaches-really-mean-239. Accessed 6 June 2011

42. Leydon J (2008) Information security breaches quadrupled in 2007. http://www.theregister.co.uk/2008/01/02/data_breaches_skyrocket/. Accessed 2 Jan 2008

43. Lisbon Treaty (TFEU). http://europa.eu/lisbon_treaty/index_en.htm. Accessed 21 Oct 2011

44. Lloyd I (2008) Information technology law, 4th edn. Oxford University Press, Oxford

45. LSE (2010) Study on the economic benefits of PETS, final report to the European Commission, dated July 2010. http://ec.europa.eu/justice/policies/privacy/docs/studies/final_report_pets_16_07_10_en.pdf

46. Matwyshyn AM (ed) (2009) Harboring data: information security, law, and the corporation. Stanford University Press, Stanford

47. Martinez J (2013) Tech associations raise concerns with EU's proposed cybersecurity rules. http://thehill.com/blogs/hillicon-valley/technology/281783-tech-associations-raise-concerns-with-eus-proposed-cybersecurity-rules. Accessed 7 Feb 2013

48. Murray A (2010) Information technology law. Oxford University Press, Oxford

49. O'Connell M (2012) Cyber security without cyber war. J Confl Sec Law 17(2):187

50. Orrick (2013) Data protection alert. http://www.orrick.com/fileupload/2389.pdf. Accessed 4 Jan 2013

51. Outlaw News (2011) Communication providers should log personal data security breaches monthly, Information Commissioner says. http://www.out-law.com/en/articles/2011/december/communications-providers-should-log-personal-data-security-breaches-monthly-information-commissioner-says/. Accessed 12 Dec 2011

52. Muge-Kinacioglu (2005) The principle of non-intervention at the United Nations: the Charter framework and the legal debate. Perceptions 10:15–39

53. NCSL (2012) Security breach notification legislations/laws. http://www.ncsl.org/issues-research/telecommunications-information-technology/security-breach-notification-laws.aspx. Accessed 6 Feb 2012

54. Rid T, McBurney P (2012) Cyber-weapons. Rusi J 157(1):6–13. http://www.tandfonline.com/doi/pdf/10.1080/03071847.2012.664354

55. Romanosky S, Telang R, Acquisti A (2011) Do data breach disclosure laws reduce identity theft? J Policy Anal Manag 2011. http://papers.ssrn.com/sol3/papers.cfm?abstract_id=1268926. Accessed 9 Feb 2012

56. The Register (2011) ICO: NHS data security breaches are just "plain daft". http://www.theregister.co.uk/2011/10/06/nhs_data_security_breaches/. Accessed 6 Oct 2011

57. Sony data breach: 100 m reasons to beef up security. http://www.computerweekly.com/news/1280097348/Sony-data-breach-100m-reasons-to-beef-up-security. Accessed 3 May 2011

58. Treaty on the European. http://eur-lex.europa.eu/en/treaties/dat/11992M/htm/11992M.html. Accessed 21 Oct 2011

59. Winn JK (2009) Are "better" security breach notification laws possible? http://papers.ssrn.com/sol3/papers.cfm?abstract_id=1416222. Accessed 2009

60. Wolf C (2010) Big changes in EU Privacy law coming? http://www.hldataprotection.com/2010/10/articles/international-eu-privacy/big-changes-in-eu-privacy-law-coming/. Accessed 20 Oct 2010

61. Wong R (2012) Data protection: idealisms and realisms (SSRN). http://papers.ssrn.com/sol3/papers.cfm?abstract_id=1985298. Accessed 29 March 2012
62. Wong R (2011) Data protection: the future of privacy. Comput Law Sec Rev 27(1):53–57
63. Zetter K (2009) Reporting of information security breaches. In: Matwyshyn AM (ed) Harboring data: information security, law and the corporation. Stanford University Press, Stanford